RIVALRY AND RESPONSE

RIVALRY AND RESPONSE

Assessing Great Power Dynamics
in Southeast Asia

JONATHAN R. STROMSETH

Editor

BROOKINGS INSTITUTION PRESS
Washington, D.C.

Copyright © 2021
THE BROOKINGS INSTITUTION
1775 Massachusetts Avenue, N.W.
Washington, D.C. 20036
www.brookings.edu

The Brookings Institution is a private nonprofit organization devoted to research, education, and publication on important issues of domestic and foreign policy. Its principal purpose is to bring the highest quality independent research and analysis to bear on current and emerging policy problems. Interpretations or conclusions in Brookings publications should be understood to be solely those of the authors.

Library of Congress Control Number: 2020952497

ISBN 9780815739142 (pbk)
ISBN 9780815739159 (ebook)

9 8 7 6 5 4 3 2 1

Typeset in Minion Pro

Composition by Elliott Beard

Contents

Contents

Preface

The Brookings Institution launched a new trilateral initiative in 2019 with experts from Southeast Asia, Australia, and the United States to examine regional trends in the context of China's dramatic rise and escalating U.S.-China rivalry. As part of this initiative, Brookings convened an inaugural dialogue in Singapore in late 2019 in partnership with the S. Rajaratnam School of International Studies (RSIS) of Singapore and the Lowy Institute of Australia. Typically, such dialogues focus heavily on security issues, but this initiative has broadened the aperture to cover economic and governance topics as well. At the Singapore dialogue, panel discussions focused on the strategic landscape and contending visions for Southeast Asia, domestic governance trends, and economic developments and challenges, with the latter focusing especially on infrastructure. The chapters of this book reflect the papers and debates that took place at the dialogue, updated to cover recent developments, and each includes policy recommendations on possible areas of cooperation among regional partners.

Southeast Asia is a diverse and dynamic region of 650 million people that is seen by Beijing as a testing ground for its rise as a global power. It is also home to two U.S. treaty allies and is the top destination for American investment in the Indo-Pacific. As China has drawn the region closer economically and taken aggressive actions in the South China Sea, the Trump administration boldly warned regional countries that China's behavior posed a clear choice between "free" and "repressive" visions of world order. While Southeast Asian nations are responding to this great power rivalry in different ways, they also do not want to take sides between Washington and Beijing. They prefer instead to focus on multilateral co-operation, regional stability, economic growth, and sustaining an open trading environment.[1]

Meanwhile, U.S.-China rivalry has become hyper-charged under the COVID-19 pandemic. As this once-in-a-century event unfolds, foreign policy experts are speculating about the future geopolitical implications of COVID-19. Some suggest that the pandemic could reshape the global order, elevating China's position at the expense of the United States, while others are skeptical that China has the capacity to emerge as a dominant world power. Still others say the pandemic won't reshape the global order so much as accelerate history, revealing and reinforcing the fundamental characteristics of geopolitics today. In this scenario, we can expect to see a further waning of American leadership, less global cooperation, and enhanced rivalry and discord between the United States and an ascendant China.[2]

How the pandemic will ultimately affect long-term geopolitical trends is difficult to predict. However, a closer look at Southeast Asia may provide some clues. Although the pandemic does not appear to be reshaping the regional order in fundamental ways, it could well accelerate preexisting trends and bolster China's position. A key near-term variable is the sequencing of economic recovery. As China recovers faster from the outbreak, it could reinforce its already advantaged economic position, advance its strategic goals as a result, and undercut U.S. efforts to compete with Beijing in the region. But China could also face resistance and pushback, as it has encountered in Europe, if its regional diplomacy becomes increasingly hostage to nationalistic impulses and rhetoric, or if it becomes rigid in debt repayment schedules for recipient countries as they navigate through the COVID-induced economic downturn.[3]

At the trilateral dialogue in Singapore, convened just before COVID-19 emerged in Wuhan, experts from Southeast Asia were already asking tough and probing questions about the objectives of U.S. Asia strategy. For instance, Southeast Asian participants said the United States should better define the end goal of U.S. Asia policy today: Is it to reestablish preeminence, construct a new balance of power, preserve the rules-based order, or some combination of these elements? They said strategic competition should be a means to an end, not an end in itself. The Trump administration also seemed to focus exclusively on confronting China, the participants added, whereas previous U.S. administrations had used a carrot-and-stick approach with Beijing that blended competition with cooperation. They also felt U.S. policy was too concentrated on defense and security, to the detriment of diplomacy and development, allowing China to fill the soft-power vacuum and capture the narrative through its signature Belt and Road Initiative (BRI).

As the Biden administration enters the White House and begins to formulate its strategy for the region, it would do well to consider these fundamental questions and concerns as well as related recommendations that appear in the chapters of this volume. It should also recognize that the security-centric paradigm that has dominated American thinking is an outmoded or insufficient lens through which to evaluate and understand the region. Increasingly, China is achieving its strategic goals in Southeast Asia through economic statecraft, and economic and technological factors are playing a prominent role in shaping the choices of Southeast Asian leaders on critical policy issues that divide Washington and Beijing. In this context, it is not surprising that many of the recommendations in this volume focus on the economic realm.

The authors and trilateral dialogue participants recommend, for example, that the United States, Australia, Japan, and the Association of Southeast Asian Nations (ASEAN) should improve coordination of development assistance in mainland Southeast Asia, or the Lower Mekong subregion, where Chinese economic power and influence is growing so dramatically. They should also encourage China to multilateralize BRI on a project-by-project basis, mitigating strategic economic competition in the process. In addition, the United States and other donors could expand assistance to ASEAN countries for negotiating and managing large infrastructure projects, from both Chinese lenders and private investors, to promote transparency and reduce the corruption often associated with administering such endeavors.

Finally, a key theme running throughout the volume is how the region can move beyond a binary choice between the United States and China. In this connection, Southeast Asian countries could work with middle powers like Australia and Japan (admittedly a major power in economic terms) to expand middle-power agency and reduce the need for an all-or-nothing choice. Among the trilateral participants, however, there is little agreement on the feasibility of such collective action as well as doubts about whether ASEAN has the capacity to create independent strategic space as U.S.-China competition continues to grow. Some bemoan the diminishing salience of ASEAN "Centrality," the notion that ASEAN provides the central platform within which regional institutions are anchored.[4] Others say that instead of just *asserting* centrality, ASEAN leaders should devise concrete ways to play a more pivotal role in shaping the emerging regional order in the broader Indo-Pacific.

Looking ahead, policymakers will need to examine how the United States, Australia, and Japan can effectively implement an evolving trilateral infrastructure partnership in Southeast Asia, promoting high governance standards in the process. What type of projects should be pursued and where, and what is the most effective way to promote a "race-to-the-top" competition with China over infrastructure financing and project implementation? Moreover, it would be instructive to investigate what such initiatives may imply for infrastructure cooperation with China. Do they foretell a new form of geopolitical competition and a more bifurcated region, or is there still room to engage China, multilateralize BRI, and reduce strategic economic rivalry over time? These questions animate the chapters in this volume, and the authors hope they will likewise stimulate policy discussions in Washington, Canberra, and ASEAN capitals as the region gradually emerges from COVID-19.

> *Jonathan Stromseth*
> Washington, D.C.
> December 2020

Notes

1. Chan Heng Chee, "Resisting the Polarising Pull of US-China Rivalry," *The Straits Times*, June 18, 2019, https://www.straitstimes.com/opinion/resisting-the-polarising-pull-of-us-china-rivalry.

2. For examples of such analysis, see Richard Haass, "The Pandemic Will Accelerate History Rather than Reshape It," *Foreign Affairs*, April 7, 2020, https://www.foreignaffairs.com/articles/united-states/2020-04-07/pandemic-will-accelerate-history-rather-reshape-it; Kurt M. Campbell and Rush Doshi, "The Coronavirus Could Reshape the Global Order: China is Maneuvering for International Leadership as the United States Falters," *Foreign Affairs*, March 18, 2020, https://www.

foreignaffairs.com/articles/china/2020-03-18/coronavirus-could-reshape-global
-order; and Susan A. Thornton, "Fears of a Chinese Global Takeover are Greatly
Exaggerated," The Brookings Institution, April 9, 2020, https://www.brookings.edu/
blog/order-from-chaos/2020/04/09/fears-of-a-chinese-global-takeover-are-greatly
-exaggerated.

3. Jonathan Stromseth, "U.S.-China Rivalry After COVID-19: Clues and Early
Indications from Southeast Asia," *Lawfare*, May 21, 2020, https://www.lawfareblog
.com/us-china-rivalry-after-covid-19-clues-and-early-indications-southeast-asia.

4. For a discussion of ASEAN centrality, see Amitav Acharya, "The Myth of
ASEAN Centrality," *Contemporary Southeast Asia* 39, no. 2 (August 2017), https://
muse.jhu.edu/article/667776.

Acknowledgments

The editor wishes to thank Richard Bush, Ryan Hass, Mireya Solís, Lindsey Ford, Joshua Meltzer, and Michael O'Hanlon for providing insightful comments and feedback on earlier versions of this volume. He also thanks Adrien Chorn for his invaluable research assistance and careful development of the appendices, and expresses his deep appreciation to Anna Newby and Ted Reinert for their editorial support. In addition, he thanks Collin Koh, Herve Lemahieu, and especially Jennifer Mason for their assistance in organizing the October 2019 trilateral dialogue, from which this book emerged, and recognizes the extensive contributions of Joseph Liow, who co-chaired the dialogue with the editor in Singapore. Finally, he thanks Adrian Ang and Amanda Trea Phua, who served as rapporteurs at the dialogue and summarized the discussion in a clear and concise form. Both the dialogue and this volume were made possible by generous support from the Australian Department of Foreign Affairs and Trade. Brookings also recognizes generous support from the Henry Luce Foundation for its Southeast Asia program. Brookings is committed to quality, independence, and impact in all of its work. Activities supported by its donors reflect this commitment.

1

Navigating Great Power Competition in Southeast Asia

JONATHAN R. STROMSETH

INTRODUCTION

Southeast Asia has become a hotbed of strategic rivalry between China and the United States. China is asserting its influence in the region through economic statecraft and far-reaching efforts to secure its sovereignty claims in the South China Sea.[1] Under the Trump administration, the United States promoted a Free and Open Indo-Pacific (FOIP) strategy that explicitly challenged China's expanding influence, warning other countries that Beijing is practicing "predatory economics" and advancing governance concepts associated with rising authoritarianism in the region.[2] Meanwhile, the Association of Southeast Asian Nations (ASEAN) has developed its own "Outlook on the Indo-Pacific" based on inclusiveness and ASEAN Centrality, while regional powers like Japan and Australia are increasing engagement with the region through trade, investment, and deepening political and security ties.

Much is at stake for U.S. foreign policy and American interests in the region. Southeast Asia includes two U.S. allies in Thailand and the Philippines, important security partners like Singapore, and key emerging partners such as Vietnam and Indonesia. Taken together, the 10 ASEAN countries boast the third-largest population in the world at 650 million. In addition, ASEAN is the fifth-largest economy in the world with a GDP of $2.8 trillion, and the top destination for U.S. investment in the Indo-Pacific at $329 billion (more than the United States has directed to China, Japan, South Korea, and India combined). Almost 42,000 U.S. companies export to ASEAN, supporting about 600,000 jobs in the United States.[3]

U.S.-China competition has further intensified in this dynamic region since the onset of the global COVID-19 pandemic. In April 2020, during a meeting with ASEAN foreign ministers to discuss the coronavirus, U.S. Secretary of State Mike Pompeo blasted China for taking aggressive actions in the South China Sea, saying it was taking advantage of the pandemic to advance its territorial ambitions. Subsequently, in July, the United States declared for the first time that China's maritime claims in the South China Sea are "unlawful," and sent two aircraft carriers to the region to conduct military exercises.[4] China then fired missiles into the South China Sea, demonstrating the potential cost of armed conflict in the region, and initiated a series of meetings and calls with ASEAN leaders offering COVID-19 recovery aid and economic cooperation. Most recently, during a virtual summit with ASEAN foreign ministers in September, Pompeo called on ASEAN to cut business dealings with Chinese companies that "bully ASEAN coastal states in the South China Sea" by helping to construct artificial Chinese outposts in the disputed maritime region.[5]

Many Southeast Asians are apprehensive about China's strategic intentions in the context of this escalating rivalry. At the same time, regional leaders have expressed unease over the Indo-Pacific strategy of the Trump administration, which has been perceived as presenting a choice between Washington and Beijing, even if that was not the intent. Indonesian President Joko "Jokowi" Widodo has called for a vision of the Indo-Pacific that includes China, declaring that ASEAN and China have no choice but to collaborate. For his part, Singaporean Prime Minister Lee Hsien Loong has said proposals for "Indo-Pacific cooperation" are welcome if they are inclusive and deepen regional integration, but they should not undermine ASEAN arrangements or "create rival blocs, deepen fault lines or force countries to take sides."[6] In this connection, there is mounting concern in ASEAN about the increasing prominence of a quadrilateral security dialogue involving the United States, Japan, Australia, and India, also known as "the Quad," widely seen as providing a counterweight to China's growing power in the Indo-Pacific.

This overview chapter explores how these great power dynamics are reverberating throughout Southeast Asia, and how ASEAN countries and other regional partners are responding along different dimensions. The chapter begins by discussing the strategic landscape and contending visions for the region, followed by an exploration of economic developments and governance trends. The chapter also summarizes the thematic chapters that appear in this volume as well as discussions at a related trilateral dialogue, including recommendations on possible areas of cooperation among regional partners.

STRATEGIC LANDSCAPE AND CONTENDING VISIONS FOR SOUTHEAST ASIA

Setting the Scene

Since 2013, Beijing has been prioritizing a highly proactive form of "neighborhood diplomacy" with the aim of promoting a "community of common destiny" in China's neighborhood areas.[7] Economic statecraft, or the use of economic tools to pursue foreign policy goals, is fundamental to this evolving foreign policy doctrine. China is pursuing this statecraft through a host of new institutions and projects, especially the Belt and Road Initiative (BRI), an ambitious effort to strengthen infrastructure, trade, and investment links between China and other countries in the region and beyond. Prominent projects in Southeast Asia include hydropower dams, oil and gas pipelines, and extensive railway plans. China has also carried out aggressive moves to defend its expansive sovereignty claims in the South China Sea based on the "nine-dash line," its historical claim that encircles roughly 90% of the contested waters.

The Trump administration's FOIP strategy is a direct response to China's more assertive approach to the region, especially in the maritime domain. The substantive content of FOIP has emerged slowly since 2017 through an assortment of speeches, fact sheets, and op-eds written by administration officials.[8] The strategy was codified more comprehensively at the Shangri-La Dialogue in June 2019, when the Pentagon released its Indo-Pacific Strategy Report focusing on preparedness, partnerships, and promoting a networked region. The report underscores Washington's commitment to a safe, secure, prosperous, and free region, and sets out four "common principles" that all countries in the region should uphold: 1) respect for sovereignty and independence of all nations; 2) peaceful resolution of disputes; 3) free, fair, and reciprocal trade based on open investment, transparent agreements, and connectivity; and 4) adherence to international rules and norms, including those of freedom of navigation and overflight.[9] China is singled out for its aggressive and predatory behavior, particularly its militarization of the South China Sea. Beijing also uses economic leverage, influence operations, and "implied military threats to persuade other states to comply with its agenda," while seeking "regional hegemony" as a prelude to "global preeminence" over the long term.[10]

The FOIP strategy is also associated with the return of the Quad. Established in 2007, the informal grouping lost traction over the years but was revived in 2017 as President Trump launched his trade war and tech offensive against China. Its most recent ministerial meeting, convened in Tokyo in October 2020, was the first standalone gathering of the Quad as previous meetings have taken place on the sideline of other summits. In Tokyo, Pompeo expressed interest in formalizing and potentially broadening the Quad to "build out a true security network." He called this network a "fabric" that could "counter the challenge that the Chinese Communist Party presents to all of us."[11]

As the Indo-Pacific concept has taken root, Southeast Asian countries have responded with efforts to develop a more ASEAN-centric approach. These efforts, led by Indonesia, came to fruition in June 2019 when ASEAN released its "ASEAN Outlook on the Indo-Pacific" (AOIP) at the 34th ASEAN Summit in Bangkok. Key themes reflected in the AOIP document are inclusiveness, economic development and connectivity, and ASEAN Centrality.[12] To this end, the document called for an "inclusive regional architecture" while emphasizing that ASEAN-led mechanisms like the East Asia Summit (EAS) should serve as platforms for dialogue and implementation of Indo-Pacific cooperation. Analysis from regional policy experts reflect concerns that the U.S. Indo-Pacific strategy is not only anti-China, but is dismissive of ASEAN, despite regular statements from the Trump administration voicing support for ASEAN Centrality. These concerns have been exacerbated by the revival of the Quad, triggering worries about how ASEAN fits into broader Indo-Pacific arrangements.

MAP 1-1. **Map of the Indo-Pacific**

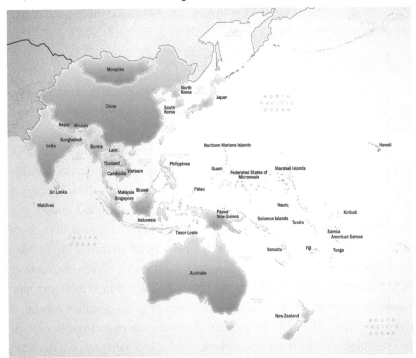

Source: Modified from "USINDOPACOM Area of Responsibility," USINDOPACOM, https://www.pacom.mil/About-USINDOPACOM/USPACOM-Area-of-Responsibility/.

In Australia's assessment, meanwhile, China's rapid growth is accelerating shifts in the relative economic and strategic weight of different countries in the Indo-Pacific, according to the government's 2017 "Foreign Policy White Paper." In Southeast Asia, for instance, the white paper notes that "China's power and influence are growing to match, and in some cases exceed, that of the United States." As competition for influence sharpens in the region, Canberra is determined to remain a leading economic and strategic partner of ASEAN and its member states, with the goal of supporting "an increasingly prosperous, outwardly-focused, stable and resilient Southeast Asia."[13] Prime Minister Scott Morrison has also affirmed that Australia's "vision of the Indo-Pacific has ASEAN at its core."[14] Additionally, Australia has a substantial interest in the stability of the South China Sea and the norms and laws that govern this international waterway. Alongside these policies for Southeast Asia, Canberra is stepping up its engagement with the Pacific Islands and Timor-Leste. In this connection, it supports Timor-Leste's ambition to join ASEAN and achieve greater economic engagement with the region.[15]

Strategic Landscape Chapters

In the thematic chapters on this topic, three scholars reflect on the above trends with special attention to the policies and challenges of their own country or region.

In chapter 2, focusing on the Trump administration's FOIP strategy, Brookings scholar Lindsey Ford notes that the administration actually sustained most of the traditional building blocks of U.S. Asia strategy—such as promoting economic prosperity, encouraging good governance and shared principles, and creating security through a network of regional allies and partners. Yet, these aspects of the FOIP narrative "have been over-shadowed and at times undermined by broader muscle movements in U.S. foreign policy, including the downward spiral in U.S.-China relations and the president's own erratic instincts on alliance policy and international trade." The administration's persistent use of punitive economic tools—notably investment restrictions, tariffs, and sanctions—have overwhelmed its narrative about free and open economic relations, Ford writes. In addition, while the administration's determination to push back more actively against China has become a rare point of bipartisan consensus in the U.S. Congress, it has also engendered regional perceptions that FOIP is more focused on containing China than on promoting stability and prosperity. As a result, close partners like South Korea and ASEAN "have been reluctant to fully endorse the Free and Open Indo-Pacific concept or be seen as aligning too closely with FOIP-branded initiatives."

Writing from a Southeast Asian perspective, analyst and academic Richard Heydarian asserts in chapter 3 that China's rise over the past decade has represented both a rapid shift in the regional balance of power and a direct assault on the legitimacy of the U.S.-led liberal international order. China is not only introducing ambitious multilateral economic initiatives like BRI, but is also expanding its military muscle through land reclamation and weaponization of artificial islands in the South China Sea. He describes the U.S. FOIP strategy as a combination of diplomatic pressure, economic cooperation, and deepening military countermeasures vis-à-vis China, carried out in tandem with like-minded powers that are likewise perturbed by Beijing's challenge to the existing order. As he notes, however, the Indo-Pacific and FOIP discourse is often viewed skeptically in Southeast Asia as a thinly veiled containment strategy against China by Washington and the other members of the Quad.[16] ASEAN categorically rejects any narrow definition of China as a hegemonic threat that has to be contained by a counter-coalition of powers, and instead sees Beijing as an "indispensable stakeholder" that should be engaged on an institutionalized, if not conciliatory, basis through ASEAN mechanisms.

In this evolving regional context, Heydarian views the AOIP as a defensive attempt at reasserting ASEAN centrality. But instead of just asserting centrality, ASEAN should also achieve and earn a pivotal role in shaping the emerging 21st-century order in the Indo-Pacific. The reality, he writes, is that ASEAN's refusal to choose on key geopolitical issues "represents a choice itself, potentially leading to its peripherality in regional affairs."

Finally, in chapter 4, Herve Lemahieu of the Lowy Institute explores Australia's unique role as a middle power that bridges the Pacific, where it is the dominant resident power, and Southeast Asia, where it must work with and through equals. Far from being hapless victims, middle powers will become increasingly important in an age of great power competition. When two superpowers are gridlocked, he writes, "the actions of the next rung of powers will constitute the marginal difference," and the fate of the regional order (or disorder) will be determined by "the interests and choices of a 'long tail' of large and small powers in managing the ups and downs of U.S.-China competition." Furthermore, since neither the United States or China can dominate the other in the Indo-Pacific, middle powers like Australia have an opportunity to cooperate with Southeast Asian countries to build an inclusive alternative to both Sino-centric and U.S.-led versions of regional order.

Lemahieu is concerned, however, that Australia's signature foreign policy initiative since 2018—the Pacific Step-up—has come at the cost of a "Southeast Asia step back." Amid growing concerns about China and a marked deterioration in Australia-China relations during the COVID-19 pandemic, Canberra should prioritize a broader and more ambitious regional strategy rather than withdrawing into a defensive "inner ring" in the Pacific. What is needed, he writes, is a more nuanced approach to working with the middle powers of Southeast Asia—one that "takes greater stock of their development needs, and is not exclusively couched in term of competition with China." Canberra should also commit to a post-pandemic recovery strategy for Southeast Asia, while facilitating cross-regional linkages between Southeast Asia and the Pacific to help diversify the international relations of Pacific island nations and minimize the risk that they become overly dependent on China.

Trilateral Discussions and Recommendations

U.S. Asia policy: These chapters also reflect discussions and debates among trilateral dialogue participants about U.S. policy, middle-power agency, and ASEAN's capacity and role, among other topics. On U.S. Asia policy, ASEAN participants are troubled that it had become too narrowly focused on China, forcing Southeast Asian countries into a binary choice that they do not want to make. The Trump administration seemed to be focused exclusively on confronting China, they believe, while previous U.S. administrations had used a carrot-and-stick approach with Beijing that combined competition with cooperation. They also feel U.S. policy is too focused on defense and security, to the detriment of diplomacy and development, permitting China to fill the soft-power vacuum and capture the narrative through the BRI.

Binary choice and middle-power agency: Several trilateral participants also believe it is time for the region to move beyond a binary choice between the United States and China. At one level, this can be accomplished by disaggregating strategic competition issue by issue. Such an approach would allow for issue-based agency by individual countries in the region. Countries can maintain close security ties with the United States, for instance, while also having close economic ties with China. At another level is the broader question of middle-power agency, collective action, and the role and capacity of ASEAN. In other words, Southeast Asian countries can work with middle powers like Australia and Japan (admittedly a major power in economic terms) to expand middle-power agency and reduce the need for an all-or-nothing choice between China and the United States. Participants disagree about the feasibility of facilitating such collective or multilateral action, with one calling it "middle-power romanticism," while others think it may be realistic in discreet issue areas like choices over 5G technology.

ASEAN's role and capacity: Participants are also divided on whether ASEAN can itself function as a middle power or has the capacity to create independent strategic space in the region in the face of escalating U.S.-China rivalry. Some argue that ASEAN is currently confronting the gravest institutional crisis in its history. The association only experienced this level of great power competition when it had five or six members during the Cold War, but not since it has expanded to ten.[17] Not surprisingly, the current geopolitical push and pull is exposing internal fissures in the larger grouping that are challenging ASEAN's consensus model of decisionmaking. Other participants, however, feel that ASEAN does not need to take sides and can overcome the present challenges by asserting ASEAN centrality.

In addition to discussing these issues, the trilateral discussions generated recommendations for possible cooperation among regional partners, or for the partners individually. These recommendations either appeared in the papers or came up in discussions, generally reflecting the perspectives of individual participants. They do not represent a consensus among the trilateral participants as a whole. Recommendations on strategic issues include:

- **Clarify U.S. policy goals:** As noted in the preface, Washington should better define the end goal of U.S. Asia policy today: Is it to reestablish preeminence, construct a new balance of power, preserve the rules-based order, or some combination of these elements? Strategic competition should be a means to an end, not an end in itself. In addition, all parties should consider what a multipolar world might look like in Asia and what their respective roles would be within it.[18]

- **Exchange candid assessments on China:** Washington and its partners should engage in more open and candid exchanges about how each country is managing the areas of cooperation and competition in its relationship with China. This will become increasingly important as the areas of rivalry and competition grow between Washington and Beijing. The United States needs to understand where partner priorities differ from its own, and why. At the same time, U.S. partners would benefit from a deeper understanding of U.S. policy, to help assuage combined concerns about abandonment and entrapment.[19]

■ **Operationalize middle-power agency and regional cooperation:** To advance middle-power agency, middle powers need to become more proactive in developing alternative approaches to addressing regional challenges, such as the provision of public goods like infrastructure finance. At the same time, regional partners such as Australia and the United States should focus trilateral coordination less on external security and more on helping ASEAN achieve its sustainable economic development goals. For this to occur, partners outside of Southeast Asia need clearer guidance from ASEAN countries about the type of public goods they are looking for and where they prefer to find them.

■ **Advance ASEAN centrality:** ASEAN centrality cannot just be claimed; it has to be earned. To facilitate, ASEAN should conduct a formal dialogue to flesh out what this concept actually means in the current regional context and how to achieve it in practical terms. Alternatively, or perhaps in parallel, ASEAN countries could pursue new forms of minilateralism, whereby core, likeminded Southeast Asian countries adopt more expedient and

Malaysia's Transport Minister Anthony Loke Siew Fook (third from left) and China ambassador to Malaysia Bai Tian (third from right), gesture during the relaunch of the East Coast Rail Link (ECRL) project in Dungun, Terengganu, Malaysia, July 25, 2019.
REUTERS/Lim Huey Teng

robust responses to shared threats, including in cooperation with external powers.[20]

■ **Engage individual Southeast Asian countries in their own right, not as a part of plan to counterbalance China:** There is an increasing tendency for security analysts in Washington, Canberra, and other Western capitals to see the relationship with ASEAN nations through the lens of competition with China. This is a mistake. As they struggle with profound historical tensions and domestic challenges, these countries often see their biggest challenges coming from inside, not outside. The best way to develop effective partnerships is thus to help them tackle their domestic challenges, not to push them to take on an international role with which they are uncomfortable.[21]

■ **Encourage ASEAN-Pacific Dialogue:** ASEAN and the Pacific Islands Forum (PIF) should develop a formal Dialogue Partnership, institutionalizing cross-regional dialogue and cooperation between their international secretariats. A number of ASEAN member states are already Dialogue Partners to the PIF. Both organizations also have a Dialogue Partnership with the European Union, which is helping to build greater understanding of the potential for enhanced multilateral governance in their regions.[22]

ECONOMIC DEVELOPMENTS AND CHALLENGES

Setting the Scene

According to the Asian Development Bank (ADB), Southeast Asian economies will need $210 billion per year in infrastructure investment from 2016 to 2030 just to keep up the momentum of economic growth.[23] In this context, Japan and China are by far the largest bilateral infrastructure financiers in Southeast Asia. Data compiled by Lowy scholar Roland Rajah indicate that China's financial commitments for infrastructure projects totaled $42 billion from 2008 to 2016, compared to $37 billion for Japan.[24] Meanwhile, recent data from Fitch Solutions indicate that Japanese-backed projects in the region's six largest economies—Indonesia, Malaysia, the Philippines, Singapore, Thailand, and Vietnam—are valued at $367 billion, compared to China's tally of $255 billion, although Fitch only counts pending projects, or those at the stages of planning a feasibility study, tender, and currently under construction.[25]

Chinese economic activities are particularly conspicuous in mainland Southeast Asia, where Beijing has cultivated the Lancang-Mekong Cooperation (LMC) mechanism to coordinate BRI projects and advance its economic and political ambitions in this critical subregion on China's immediate periphery. Established in 2015 among the six countries that comprise the Greater Mekong subregion (Cambodia, China, Laos, Myanmar, Thailand, and Vietnam), the LMC promotes cooperation across a range of economic and cultural domains, but the driving force is infrastructure.[26] Beijing has set aside over $22 billion under the mechanism to support projects focusing on technological connectivity and industrial development as well as trade, agriculture, and poverty alleviation. In Laos, for instance, Beijing is bankrolling the $7 billion China-Laos railway project, extending almost 260 miles from the Chinese border to Vientiane, a project that amounts to almost half the country's gross domestic product (GDP).[27]

The strategic implications of China's dam building along the Mekong are particularly daunting. China has built eleven mega-dams along the upper Mekong within China, apart from the hydropower dams it is financing in Laos and Cambodia, effectively giving it the power to "turn off the tap" for the five ASEAN countries that rely on the river for economic stability and security in the Lower Mekong subregion. A recent study from U.S.-based climate consultant Eyes on Earth has offered evidence that Chinese dams held back water in 2019—exacerbating drought in Vietnam, Laos, Cambodia, and Thailand.[28]

China's rising economic influence has generated unease and pushback in Southeast Asia over contract terms, corruption, and possible debt traps. However, as reflected in Malaysia's successful renegotiation of the Chinese-financed East Coast Rail Link project in 2019, ASEAN countries appear to be getting smarter in the way they are managing BRI and negotiating with China.[29] Beijing is also showing a capacity to learn from its implementation mistakes, make adjustments, and preempt criticism from the region going forward. In sum, there appears to be a mutual learning dynamic at play that could make BRI more resilient and enduring in Southeast Asia over time.[30] Not surprisingly, Southeast Asian policy experts, businesspeople, and other stakeholders have an acute awareness and recognition of China's growing economic influence in the region, as reflected in Figure 1, even as they remain wary of its long-term strategic intentions.

FIGURE 1-1. **In your view, which country/regional organization has the most influential economic power in Southeast Asia?**

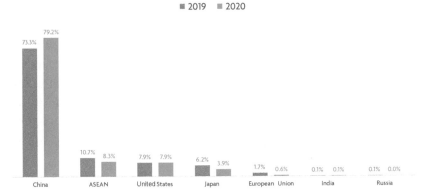

Source: The State of Southeast Asia: 2019 and 2020 Survey Reports (Singapore: ASEAN Studies Center, ISEAS-Yusof Ishak Institute, January 2019 and January 2020), http://www.iseas.edu.sg/images/pdf/TheStateofSEASurveyReport_2019. pdf and http://www.iseas.edu.sg/images/pdf/TheStateofSEASurveyReport_2020.pdf.

Finally, China's economic advance has encouraged other countries to reform and step up their own infrastructure plans for the region. The United States has transformed the Overseas Private Investment Corporation (OPIC) into the new International Development Finance Agency (DFC), doubling OPIC's $30 billion investment ceiling to $60 billion, while Australia has revamped its export credit agency, now called Export Finance Australia, giving it more leeway to finance overseas infrastructure projects. In late 2018, Australia and the United States also joined Japan to form a Trilateral Partnership for Infrastructure Investment in the Indo-Pacific in order to promote sustainable infrastructure based on high standards—notably good governance, open procurement, debt sustainability, and environmental and social safeguards. More recently, in November 2019, the three countries launched the Blue Dot Network, a multi-stakeholder initiative designed to evaluate and certify nominated infrastructure projects based on high quality standards and principles.[31] Another key goal of these initiatives is to incentivize private-sector financing for infrastructure development throughout the region.

Economic Chapters

In chapter 5, Brookings scholar David Dollar investigates these developments by examining U.S. and Chinese infrastructure initiatives in Southeast Asia, seeking to combat common misconceptions and unsubstantiated rhetoric. Investing in infrastructure is a crucial aspect of a successful growth strategy, Dollar says, and traditionally ASEAN countries could rely on Western support through bilateral financing and multilateral development banks. However, Japan is now the only significant financier among Western donors. From 2015 to 2017, Japan committed $13 billion to transport and energy infrastructure in ASEAN countries, whereas no other donor reached $1 billion per year in these sectors.[32] Meanwhile, China is rapidly expanding its infrastructure financing under BRI through two policy banks, the China Development Bank and the Export-Import Bank of China, motivated by both economic and strategic considerations.

Since China's money is mostly non-concessional, Dollar writes, Beijing has been accused of "debt-trap diplomacy"—that is, of saddling countries with higher-interest debt that they are unable to repay, giving China leverage over the borrowing country. However, looking at the data on external debt relative to gross national income (GNI) for ASEAN countries, he finds that most are in very good shape as of 2018. The exceptions are Laos, with an external debt to GNI of 90%, and, to a lesser extent, Cambodia at 68%. Laos highlights the risk of taking on too much debt too quickly, especially non-concessional debt, a problem exacerbated by the economic distress brought on by COVID-19. Dollar notes that Laos is eligible for the Debt Service Suspension Initiative promoted by the G20, but has chosen instead to negotiate directly with China, its main creditor, including a debt-for-equity swap in which the China Southern Power Grid Co. is taking a direct stake in Laos's power transmission company.

Continuing with the infrastructure theme, Roland Rajah examines in chapter 6 the renewed interest of the United States and Australia in the sustainable infrastructure agenda in Southeast Asia, and in coordinating their expanded and revamped infrastructure efforts with Japan. According to Rajah, the current approach of these partners is unlikely to provide a credible response or alternative to China's Belt and Road Initiative. The emphasis on mobilizing more private capital for infrastructure development, for instance, simply cannot deliver the dividends needed to compete with the scale of BRI. Nor is an emphasis on high infrastructure standards likely to deter Southeast Asian governments from pursuing Chinese projects as long as China continues to be perceived as offering faster, less risk-averse, and more responsive support compared to alternatives available from traditional partners. Facing these challenges, says Rajah, the trilateral partners need to improve the competitiveness of their own infrastructure approaches to be more streamlined and fit-for-purpose. More ambition is needed as well. Contrary to the assumption that it is impossible to match China's financing scale, Rajah argues that the gap is actually not insurmountable and a moderate increase in official development assistance would be enough for the trilateral partners to keep pace.

Lastly, in chapter 7, Khuong Minh Vu of the Lee Kuan Yew School of Public Policy reviews the performance of ASEAN countries over the two decades since the Asian financial crisis in the late 1990s, as well as the countries' vulnerabilities to the U.S.-China trade war and the COVID-19 pandemic. He argues that these crises show that the world has reached an inflection point, requiring fundamental change in development thinking and approaches. This message is particularly relevant for ASEAN countries, which had made impressive economic achievements before

U.S., Australia, Japan delegation travels to indonesia
to explore investment opportunities—
U.S. embassy and consulates in Indonesia, August 28, 2019

https://id.usembassy.gov/u-s-australia-japan-delegation-travels-to-indonesia-to-explore-investment-opportunities/.

the COVID-19 outbreak. As all ASEAN countries have established aspirational goals for their development journeys over the next two to three decades, Vu says that "they should turn these emerging threats into a unique opportunity to raise the sense of urgency for change and deepen their commitment to fundamental and visionary reform efforts," so as to be highly "prepared, competitive, and resilient" in the future development landscape. Furthermore, ASEAN will be stronger if it can position itself as an integrated market and a well-coordinated community, in which each country endeavors to enhance not only its own fitness, but also the fitness of the region in the post-COVID-19 global economic evolution.

Trilateral Discussion and Recommendations

Japan's role in the region: A key theme in this topic area is Southeast Asia's high regard and appreciation for Japan's role in the region, especially in the infrastructure domain. In the words of one participant: "Japan asks little but provides a lot." Japan is also seen as well-resourced, flexible, inclusive, and is willing to cooperate with China. When Prime Minister Shinzo Abe visited China in October 2018, for instance, fifty-two memoranda of understanding (MOUs) were announced, encouraging business cooperation in third-country markets in such fields as transportation, energy, and health care. Although implementation remains a work in progress, the MOUs have signaled to ASEAN countries that Japan is willing to engage China, and that its Indo-Pacific strategy is qualitatively different from the U.S. version.[33] According to the above-noted ISEAS survey, moreover, Japan is the most trusted major power in the region, with 61.2% of respondents indicating that they are confident or very confident that Japan will "do the right thing" to contribute to global peace, security, prosperity, and governance. Japan is the only major power to achieve an overall trust level above 50% in the 2020 survey, followed by the European Union (38%), the United States (30.3%), China (16.1%), and India (16%).

Politicization of aid and development: Trilateral participants are concerned that development assistance is increasingly becoming a proxy for great power competition in Southeast Asia. This requires recipient countries to factor in geopolitical considerations when deciding whether to accept or decline infrastructure financing, often causing them to hedge. The competition is most conspicuous and tangible in mainland Southeast Asia, or the Lower Mekong subregion, where China is promoting the LMC; the United States is supporting its new Mekong-U.S. Partnership, an expansion of the Lower Mekong Initiative (LMI); and Washington and Tokyo recently launched the Japan-U.S. Mekong Power Partnership (JUMPP). The trilateral infrastructure partnership of Japan, Australia, and the United States also appears to be eyeing this area. One participant describes the Mekong subregion as a "spaghetti bowl" of separate aid initiatives with little coordination between them. Participants encourage the United States and Australia to design and support development projects that Mekong countries actually want, urging them to better align their projects with homegrown initiatives, such as the Ayeyawady-Chao Phraya-Mekong Economic Cooperation Strategy (ACMECS).

Recommendations on economic issues include:

■ **Improve coordination of development assistance in the Mekong**: The United States, Australia, and ASEAN are all engaging in the Mekong through different dialogue mechanisms. They should explore opportunities to better align their approaches by exchanging information on their respective activities, sharing country-level needs assessments, and developing coordinated initiatives on water and resource management.[34]

■ **Encourage the World Bank to focus more on infrastructure**: The World Bank should focus more on infrastructure and reduce processing times for its loans, giving developing countries competitive alternatives. In addition, multilateral development banks should assist ASEAN governments to consider and manage BRI projects, using existing infrastructure advisory facilities to provide technical assistance.[35]

■ **Dial down anti-China rhetoric and join AIIB (United States and Japan)**: U.S. accusations of China's "debt-trap diplomacy" do not resonate with much of the developing world and make the United States look insecure. Meanwhile, the Asian Infrastructure Investment Bank (AIIB) is transparent and multilateral and should be encouraged as an alternative to Chinese bilateral financing. Joining AIIB would demonstrate that Washington and Tokyo are not simply opposing all Chinese external efforts; it would also give credence to legitimate Western criticisms of China's bilateral programs.[36]

■ **Multilateralize BRI:** The United States, Japan, and regional countries should encourage China to multilateralize BRI on a project-by-project basis, mitigating strategic economic competition in the process. Growing economic challenges in China, coupled with increased borrowing and heightened risk, could persuade Beijing to move in this direction.

■ **Strike a balance between high standards and efficiency in infrastructure financing:** The current focus of the trilateral partners on "high standards" may prove ineffective in competing with China's BRI. Efforts to streamline processes and strike a better balance between managing risk and delivering results are needed. This could provide a useful agenda for the Blue Dot Network.[37]

GOVERNANCE TRENDS IN SOUTHEAST ASIA

Setting the Scene

The conventional wisdom among Southeast Asia watchers is that democracy has been declining in the region for several years. Observers point to the military coup in Thailand in 2014, President Rodrigo Duterte's drug war and extrajudicial killings in the Philippines, Prime Minister Hun Sen's dissolution of opposition parties and muzzling of the media in Cambodia, and the rise of religious and political intolerance in Indonesia. Even the glow of Aung San Suu Kyi's historic electoral victory in Myanmar in 2015, ending decades of outright military rule, is fading as nearly 750,000 Rohingya Muslims have fled to Bangladesh to escape ethnic cleansing by the Myanmar military. This "democratic decline," or "regression to authoritarianism," is typically attributed to such chronic problems as political corruption, weak electoral systems, and high levels of inequality.[38]

Alongside these broader trends, Southeast Asian countries are now also coping with the significant governance challenges of responding to the COVID-19 pandemic. Viewed as a success story early in the crisis, the region was experiencing persistent and accelerating infections in several nations by fall of 2020. ASEAN countries had reported a cumulative 1,271,003 cases as of early December, with Indonesia and the Philippines comprising 81% of the total. While these numbers pale in comparison to those seen in the United States, India, and other regions, tens of thousands of infections are likely going undetected due to low testing rates, especially in Indonesia, which has the world's fourth-largest population of over 270 million. The administration of President Jokowi has struggled to respond effectively to the contagion, implementing inconsistent lockdowns and minimal contacting tracing. Indonesia's testing rate is also among the lowest in the world.[39]

Despite sharing an 800-mile border with China, Vietnam's response has been far more effective owing to a combination of early and decisive action, extensive surveillance, mass mobilization, and effective use of social media to publicize regulations and programs related to the pandemic. It has also carried out intricate and multilayered contact-tracing procedures.[40] As of December 8, 2020, this country of nearly 100,000 million had recorded only 1,377 cases and 35 deaths. While observers have attributed Vietnam's success to its authoritarian political system and toolkit, it also appears to have resulted from decades-long reforms aimed at improving governance and responsiveness at local levels—including steady advances in information access, corruption control, and healthcare—as well as improvements in central-local policy coordination.[41] Although Vietnam experienced a minor flare-up in cases in late July and August, the government subsequently reestablished control over the pandemic. Efforts are now underway to gradually reopen the economy, which is projected to grow by 1.8% in 2020. All of the other major ASEAN economies are expected to remain in negative territory.

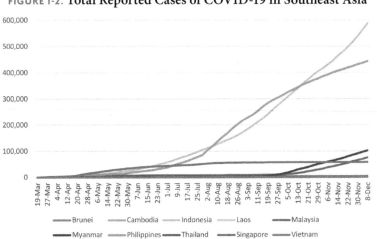

FIGURE 1-2. **Total Reported Cases of COVID-19 in Southeast Asia**

Source: Johns Hopkins University

Meanwhile, as discussed extensively at the trilateral dialogue, Southeast Asia is also witnessing a dramatic rise of Chinese power and influence throughout the region, as well as a significant escalation of U.S.-China rivalry. Analysis of this growing rivalry has focused largely on the security realm and divergent efforts to define the broader regional order. However, the evolving "pull of power" from Beijing and Washington may also be affecting political trends in individual Southeast Asian countries as China exemplifies, and perhaps even propagates, a political model that could appeal to leaders seeking economic growth opportunities without commensurate political liberties or constraints on their power.[42] The chapters on this topic consider the potential impact of China's rise on governance trends in the region, as compared to internal drivers and historical factors inherent to the countries themselves.

Governance Chapters

In chapter 8, Lowy scholar Ben Bland set the stage for this topic by investigating the intersection between contemporary governance challenges and long-standing historical tensions in Southeast Asia. While analysts and academics often ascribe the recent challenges to sweeping trends like the spread of divisive social media or the increasing appeal of China's authoritarian model, Bland argues that it is more instructive to see the problems in their own unique historical context. In particular, he argues that many of the major governance problems faced by countries in the region—including Indonesia, Malaysia, Myanmar, the Philippines, and Thailand—are "the result of long-running tensions, which in some cases date back to the late colonial era and the struggle for independence." For example, Indonesia has developed remarkably resilient, free and fair elections since the fall of Suharto in 1998, but according to Bland, it has failed to reform its political system to curb the dominance of Suharto-era elites. Indonesia is also still struggling to resolve the relationship between Islam and the state, a conundrum that dates back to its origins as an independent nation in 1945.

Bland also sees these themes reflected in Indonesia's response to COVID-19. While often disregarding experts in public health, President Jokowi has looked to the military and police to lead the response. Indonesia is not faring well, as noted above, with a rising caseload and a government that has failed to set out a clear strategy for tackling the twin health and economic crises. This approach reveals "the enduring power of the military, more than two decades after the post-Suharto reforms that ended its 'dual function' role in civilian government." It also underlines the persistence of authoritarian figures and authoritarian thinking in the Indonesian government. Although the president is not actively trying to roll back democracy, Bland writes, he is reaching for the levers of power that he thinks will deliver quick results.

In a related trilateral paper, Philips Vermonte of the Centre for Strategic and International Studies (CSIS) Indonesia delved further into the Indonesian case by analyzing different trends and challenges that are affecting the process of democratic consolidation in the country. He notes that the April 2019 elections—which resulted in the reelection of Jokowi for a second term—should have been a propitious sign since it was Indonesia's fourth direct presidential election and fifth parliamentary election since the country democratized in 1999. Yet, Vermonte points to recent political developments suggesting that Indonesia is far from a consolidated democracy today. These developments include the rise of identity politics, seen most vividly during the 2017 Jakarta gubernatorial election, when incumbent governor Basuki Tjahaya Purnama (Ahok), a non-Javanese Christian of Chinese descent, faced a debilitating smear campaign from conservative Muslim groups that invoked religious and racial sentiment. Counterbalancing this trend, however, is the rise of technocratic governors at the provincial level, suggesting that Indonesian voters are also looking for leaders focused on better governance and improved public service delivery.

Vermonte concludes on a pessimistic note, pointing out that successful economic growth in China and other non-Western economies has not been associated with democratic development and freedom. "What can spell trouble for developing countries like Indonesia," he writes, "is that China might inspire and even be used as a working model that a certain level of economic development is indeed possible without opting for democracy."

Finally, in chapter 9, Thomas Pepinsky of Cornell University widens the aperture and provides a panoramic overview of governance trends in Southeast Asia, offering two main findings based on existing empirical data. First, he finds no evidence of region-wide democratic erosion in either the short or medium term. Cases of democratic regression like Thailand have been matched by cases of opening and liberalization in Myanmar and Timor-Leste, however halting and incomplete. Other regularly cited cases of democratic backsliding, such as Cambodia under Hun Sen or the Philippines under Rodrigo Duterte, are "simply the latest iterations of medium-term political processes specific to each country." Second, Pepinsky finds little correspondence between democratic practices and civil liberties, on the one hand, and effective and capable governance, on the other. In other words, Southeast Asia as a region "is characterized by a decoupling of governance and regime type." Governance indicators for Thailand have remained roughly constant, for instance, despite dramatic political change on multiple occasions.

Pepinsky recognizes that China's rise is an inescapable reality for politicians and mass publics alike in Southeast Asia, and notes that the decoupling of democracy and governance could provide an opening for the "Beijing model" to take root in the region. With regard to COVID-19, for instance, a key point to watch is whether Southeast Asian countries focus on the U.S. narrative of culpability or the Chinese narrative of effective management. But for Pepinsky, China's economic policies and diplomatic actions are not directly encouraging authoritarian capitalism or incentivizing countries to follow a particular national political or economic model. Instead, China's primary objective for Southeast Asian countries is to "establish and maintain regional dominance, which is best accomplished by working with governments of any type within the region and pushing for issues in China's strategic interest (that is, megaprojects, dams, South China Sea)."

Trilateral Discussion and Recommendations

China model: In this subject area, Southeast Asian participants see little evidence that China is actively promoting a new political model in the region based on authoritarianism or state capitalism, but they note that China is trying to undermine the appeal of the Western democratic model by highlighting its flaws. Additionally, although Beijing may have stepped up efforts to influence domestic outcomes or public opinion in Southeast Asia, this was being done to promote Chinese strategic interests in the region or to bolster the position of the Chinese Communist Party at home.

Indirect effects: Some participants detect indirect effects of China's growing influence on governance trends in the region. In other words, even if China is not proactively promoting an authoritarian model of development, it might still be reinforcing authoritarian tendencies or inhibiting democratic consolidation in some countries through the export of surveillance technologies, expansion of its state media footprint, or provision of financial support through development aid, infrastructure investments, and other modalities.

Socializing with Southeast Asia: Finally, participants observe that China is "socializing" with ASEAN countries to an increasing degree, sending a continuous flow of missions and groups to the region in recent years. The Chinese "are in listening mode compared to five years ago," notes one participant, even contracting local think tanks to conduct studies on BRI implementation experiences, warts and all.

Recommendations on governance issues include:

- **Take the long view:** The current governance challenges make it hard for Australia, the United States, and other Western governments to deepen engagement with ASEAN countries, especially as China expands its influence in the region. Still, Western governments should not succumb to resignation in the face of seemingly intractable problems; rather, they should endeavor to better understand the historical roots of Southeast Asia's contemporary governance issues, craft their assistance accordingly, and commit for the long term.[43]

- **Approach governance reform and democracy promotion separately:** Instead of trying to re-couple democracy and accountability within Southeast Asia, based on the hypothesis that one will produce the other, it is important to acknowledge their decoupling and treat each as a separate issue worth pursuing in its own right. Donors looking to promote accountability, for instance, can look for areas of agreement with local counterparts, such as transparent frameworks, dispute-resolution procedures, and data transparency. In terms of democracy, it is important to recognize that Southeast Asians desire democratic rights for the same reasons as others around the world: because these rights provide voice and allow citizens to advocate for their own civil liberties.[44]

- **Promote transparency in infrastructure investments:** In connection with the economic discussion above, the United States and other donors should continue to offer assistance to select ASEAN countries in negotiating and managing large infrastructure projects, from both Chinese lenders and private investors, to encourage transparency and reduce the corruption often associated with administering such projects.

CONCLUSION

The foregoing discussion, reflecting both the chapters in this volume and discussion among the trilateral participants, offers a rich and comprehensive analysis of key challenges facing Southeast Asia amid accelerating U.S.-China rivalry. Meanwhile, as this book goes to press in December 2020, the COVID-19 crisis appears to be bolstering China's position as the country recovers faster from the pandemic. While the U.S. economy remains mired in recession, the Chinese economy is rebounding and surged by 4.9% in the third quarter of 2020 compared to the same period last year. Chinese exports and imports are growing as well, showing a recovery in trade. In fact, ASEAN has recently become China's largest trading partner—not just the other way around—eclipsing the European Union and the United States for the first time.[45]

The Chinese economy also faces serious challenges, of course, and could stumble.[46] Yet, as ASEAN governments try to recover from the pandemic, they are watching the Chinese economy closely for signs of a sustained recovery and possible knock-on effects. They recognize that China currently is the largest growth engine of the world economy, accounting for nearly 30% of global growth. ASEAN policymakers will be clear-eyed about these economic realities as they look to the future, estimate China's economic footprint, and calculate their likely interdependencies and opportunities with Beijing. These interdependencies may deepen and accelerate with the recent signing of the Regional Comprehensive Economic Partnership (RCEP), a free-trade agreement involving the ten ASEAN countries, China, Japan, Korea, Australia, and New Zealand. National University of Singapore Professor Khong Yuen Foong has aptly framed the strategic implications for ASEAN as the recovery unfolds: "I will not underestimate the United States' economic resilience and technological ingenuity, but if China were to do better on the economic front, its narrative about being the wave of the future will fall on receptive ears in Southeast Asia."[47]

However, while Beijing may reap strategic benefits from the pace and sequencing of economic recovery, it could also face trip wires if Chinese diplomacy invokes nationalistic rhetoric or aggressively pursues its territorial claims in the South China Sea. The pandemic has already spurred some anti-Chinese sentiment and activities in the region, particularly in Indonesia, which has a long history of distrust and resentment between the ethnic Chinese community and the indigenous populations.[48] On social media, Filipinos also responded angrily to a Chinese music video—titled "One Sea"—that showcases China's COVID-19 aid to the Philippines while simultaneously appearing to legitimize Chinese claims to waters that Manila views as its territory in the South China Sea. A few days before the music video was released, a Chinese warship had aimed weapons at a Philippine navy vessel near a disputed reef.[49]

This maritime assertiveness will provide a continued opening for the United States to cultivate relations with ASEAN countries in the security domain. To be effective in sustaining American power and influence, however, Washington must also improve its economic standing in a region where economic factors are playing a prominent role in shaping the decisions of Southeast Asian leaders on critical issues that divide Washington and Beijing—including the deployment of 5G technologies. This will not only require operationalizing and expanding infrastructure coordination with allies and partners, as discussed in this volume, but also developing a comprehensive economic strategy that offers a positive message for multilateral engagement with the region. The reorganization of supply chains is another important variable, which could redound to the benefit of Washington or Beijing depending on how trends unfold.

In response to the pandemic, both China and the United States have expanded aid to ASEAN countries as they battle COVID-19 and try to manage the associated economic challenges. China sent shipments of masks and ventilators to the region early in the crisis and has promised ASEAN countries that they will be among the first to receive Chinese COVID-19 vaccines once they become available. Beijing has also pledged to support Indonesia's efforts to become the center for vaccine production in Southeast Asia.[50] For its part, the Trump administration announced in September 2020 that it had provided $87 million in U.S. government assistance to fight COVID-19 in ASEAN countries under the U.S.-ASEAN Strategic Partnership. In Thailand, for instance, the U.S. Centers for Disease Control and Prevention is providing training to physicians and lab technicians on performing COVID-19 testing.[51]

As the United States and China jockey for position in the region, both countries have been diminished globally by their domestic responses to COVID-19. The aura of American competence has been punctured, and the world will ultimately remember that China muzzled the whistleblowers and allowed the virus to spread across the globe—enabled by a governance system that values centralized, personalized power over transparency.[52] Where the great powers have failed, however, middle powers have succeeded spectacularly in controlling the virus, particularly in Asia. These include democracies like South Korea and Taiwan and single-party systems like Vietnam. Their success does not appear to stem from regime type, but rather from transparent and effective governance that is guided by science—including the capacity of central authorities to mobilize and direct resources in a time of national crisis.

Finally, as Southeast Asia looks ahead to a post-COVID world, it is worth considering whether this is also a "middle-power moment" in geopolitical terms, when middle powers have a genuine opportunity to increase collaboration and influence as great power rivalry heats up in the region.[53] Will ASEAN play a central role, as it tries to navigate and manage great power competition in the region, or could we see the emergence of minilateral initiatives involving select ASEAN countries? This volume provides analysis and recommendations for policymakers as they address these questions not only in ASEAN capitals, but also in Washington, Canberra, and beyond. Grouped by subtopic, the ensuing chapters address these questions in greater depth—delving into the strategic, economic and governance challenges of a dynamic and strategic region, caught in the vortex of escalating great power competition.

Notes

1. Jonathan Stromseth, "The Testing Ground: China's Rising Influence in Southeast Asia and Regional Responses" (Washington, DC: The Brookings Institution, November 2019), https://www.brookings.edu/wp-content/uploads/2019/11/FP_20191119_china_se_asia_stromseth.pdf.

2. In a speech at the Brookings Institution in late 2019, David R. Stilwell, Assistant Secretary of State at the Bureau of East Asian and Pacific Affairs, said increasing authoritarianism is reflected in Beijing's "New Type governance idea, in the region and beyond." See Stilwell, "The U.S., China, and Pluralism in International Affairs"

(remarks, Washington, DC, December 2, 2019), http://www.state.gov/the-u-s-chinaand-pluralism-in-international-affairs/.

3. "ASEAN Matters for America / America Matters for ASEAN" (Washington, DC: East-West Center, 2019), 14–20, https://asiamattersforamerica.org/uploads/pub lications/2019-ASEAN-Matters-for-America.pdf.

4. Press Statement: "U.S. Position on Maritime Claims in the South China Sea" (U.S. Department of State, July 13, 2020), https://www.state.gov/u-s-position-on-maritime-claims-in-the-south-china-sea/.

5. For background on the events and developments discussed in this paragraph, see Grant Peck, "U.S. Blasts China at Southeast Asian Meeting on Coronavirus," Associated Press, April 23, 2020, https://apnews.com/article/1a911da2ffaab5c5 097ab52791bbf1d8; Shi Jiangtao, "China Woos ASEAN Neighbors in Bid to Avoid U .S.-led Coalition on Doorstep," *South China Morning Post*, July 29, 2020, https:// www.scmp.com/news/china/diplomacy/article/3095006/china-woos-asean-neighbours-bid-avoid-us-led-coalition-its; and "Pompeo Urges Southeast Asia to Cut Ties with 'Bully' China Firms," Bloomberg, September 9, 2020, https://www.bloomberg.com/news/articles/2020-09-10/vietnam-backs-u-s-role-in-south-china-sea-rebuffing-beijing.

6. For further analysis of these trends, see Jonathan Stromseth, "Don't Make Us Choose: Southeast Asia in the Throes of U.S.-China Rivalry" (Washington, DC: The Brookings Institution, October 2019), https://www.brookings.edu/wp-content/uploads/2019/10/FP_20191009_dont_make_us_choose.pdf.

7. During a speech to the Indonesian parliament in October 2013, Chinese President Xi Jinping referred explicitly to a shared future involving China and ASEAN: "The China-ASEAN community of shared destiny is closely linked with the ASEAN community and the East Asia community. The two sides need to bring out their respective strengths to realize diversity, harmony, inclusiveness and common progress for the benefit of the people of the region and beyond." See Xi Jinping, "Speech by Chinese President Xi Jinping to Indonesian Parliament" (speech, Beijing, October 2, 2013), http://www.asean-china-center.org/english/2013-10/03/c_133062675.htm.

8. In its current usage, "Indo-Pacific" was first put forward by Japanese Prime Minister Shinzo Abe in 2007, when he spoke of a "dynamic coupling" of the Indian and Pacific Oceans in a 2007 speech to the Indian parliament. See Jeff M. Smith, "Unpacking the Free and Open Indo-Pacific," War on the Rocks, March 14, 2018, https://warontherocks.com/2018/03/unpacking-the-free-and-open-indo-pacific.

9. "Indo-Pacific Strategy Report: Preparedness, Partnerships, and Promoting a Networked Region" (U.S. Department of Defense, June 1, 2019), 1, 3–6, https://media.defense.gov/2019/Jul/01/2002152311/-1/-1/1/DEPARTMENT-OF-DEFENSE-INDO-PACIFIC-STRATEGY-REPORT-2019.PDF.

10. Ibid., 7–9.

11. "Pompeo Aims to 'Institutionalize' Quad Ties to Counter China," *Nikkei Asia*, October 6, 2020, https://asia.nikkei.com/Editor-s-Picks/Interview/Pompeo-aims-to-institutionalize-Quad-ties-to-counter-China. For background on the origins and development of the Quad, see Tanvi Madan, "What You Need to Know

About the 'Quad,' in Charts," The Brookings Institution, October 5, 2020, https://www.brookings.edu/blog/order-from-chaos/2020/10/05/what-you-need-to-know-about-the-quad-in-charts/.

12. The Pentagon's *Indo-Pacific Strategy Report* says the "United States continues to support ASEAN centrality in the regional security architecture, and the U.S. free and open Indo-Pacific strategy seeks to further empower it" (p. 46).

13. "2017 Foreign Policy White Paper," Australian Government (November 2017), http://www.dfat.gov.au/about-us/publications/Pages/2017-foreign-policy-white-paper.

14. Scott Morrison, "Where We Live" (speech, Sydney, June 26, 2019), http://www.pm.gov.au/media/where-we-live-asialink-bloomberg-address. In this foreign policy address, Australian Prime Minister Scott Morrison said Australia-U.S. relations have never been stronger and Canberra's "alliance with the U.S. is the bedrock of Australia's security." He also said Australia's "relationship with China has many strengths," particularly in the trade domain with two-way trade reaching $215 billion in 2018.

15. "2017 Foreign Policy White Paper," Australian Government.

16. Regional perceptions of FOIP are reflected in a survey by the ISEAS-Yusof Ishak Institute in Singapore. For their 2020 survey report, released in January, ISEAS asked policy experts, businesspeople, and other stakeholders across ASEAN how they view the Indo-Pacific concept. Only 28.4% of respondents considered the Indo-Pacific concept to be a "viable option for a new regional order." Although this was up from 17.2% in their 2019 survey, the overall assessment of U.S. engagement in Southeast Asia is moving in an increasingly negative direction. In fact, respondents who think the level of U.S. engagement has either "decreased" or "decreased significantly" grew from 68% in 2019 to 77% in 2020. With respect to China, 38.2% of respondents viewed China as a "revisionist power" that "intends to turn Southeast Asia into its sphere of influence." See The State of Southeast Asia: 2020 Survey Report (Singapore: Asian Studies Center, ISEAS-Yusof Ishak Institute, January 2020), 32–39, http://www.iseas.edu.sg/images/pdf/TheStateofSEASurveyReport_2020.pdf.

17. ASEAN was founded on August 8, 1967, after the Foreign Ministers from the original five member states—Indonesia, Malaysia, the Philippines, Singapore, and Thailand—signed the ASEAN Declaration in Bangkok, Thailand. Brunei became ASEAN's sixth member in January 1984 following its independence from the United Kingdom. After the end of the Cold War in 1991, Vietnam was admitted in July 1995, Lao PDR and Myanmar in July 1997, and then finally Cambodia became ASEAN's tenth member in April 1999. See "About ASEAN," The ASEAN Secretariat, https://asean.org/asean/about-asean/.

18. In a major Asia speech delivered at the at The Brookings Institution in December 2019, Assistant Secretary of State David Stilwell said the United States welcomes "pluralism" and "multipolarity" in regional affairs and is not forcing countries to choose. See Stilwell, "The U.S., China, and Pluralism in International Affairs" (U.S. Department of State, December 2, 2019), http://www.state.gov/the-u-s-chinaand-pluralism-in-international-affairs.

19. Drawn from chapter 2 in this volume by Lindsey Ford.

20. The point on minilateralism is drawn from chapter 3 in this volume by Richard Javad Heydarian.

21. Drawn from chapter 8 in this volume by Ben Bland, who made this point with regard to Indonesia.

22. Drawn from chapter 4 in this volume by Herve Lemahieu.

23. ADB estimate cited in Michelle Jamrisko, "China No Match for Japan in Southeast Asia Infrastructure Race," Bloomberg, June 22, 2019, http://www.bloomberg.com/news/articles/2019-06-23/china-nomatch-for-japan-in-southeast-asia-infrastructure-race. See also "Meeting Asia's Infrastructure Needs" (Metro Manila: Asian Development Bank, 2017), xiv, 43, http://www.adb.org/sites/default/files/publication/227496/special-report-infrastructure.pdf.

24. Drawn from chapter 6 in this volume by Roland Rajah.

25. Jamrisko, "China No Match for Japan in Southeast Asia Infrastructure Race."

26. Pongphisoot Busbarat, "Grabbing the Forgotten: China's Leadership Consolidation in Mainland Southeast Asia through the Mekong-Lancang Cooperation," Perspective 2018, no. 7 (Singapore: ISEAS Yusof Ishak Institute, February 6, 2018), 4, https://iseas.edu.sg/images/pdf/ISEAS_Perspective_2018_7@50.pdf.

27. Jitsiree Thongnoi, "Too Little, Too Late for US 'Recommitment' to Mekong Countries? China's Already There," *South China Morning Post*, June 16, 2019, http://www.scmp.com/week-asia/politics/article/3014612/too-little-too-late-us-recommitment-mekong-countries-chinas.

28. Alan Basist and Claude Williams, "Monitoring the Quantity of Water Flowing through the Upper Mekong Basin under Natural (Unimpeded) Conditions" (Bangkok, Thailand: Sustainable Infrastructure Partnership, April 2020, https://558353b6-da87-4596-a181-b1f20782dd18.filesusr.com/ugd/81dff2_68504848510349d6a827c6a433122275.pdf?index=true.

29. In 2018, Malaysia halted this $20 billion railway project funded by China, citing the country's inability to pay. Subsequently, Malaysia renegotiated with Beijing, reduced the cost by about a third, and resumed the project. See Bhavan Jaipragas, "Malaysia To Go Ahead with China-Backed East Coast Rail link," *South China Morning Post*, April 12, 2019, http://www.scmp.com/week-asia/geopolitics/article/3005831/malaysia-decide-today-stalled-china-backed-east-coast-rail.

30. See Stromseth, "Don't Make Us Choose," for further analysis of this dynamic.

31. "The Launch of Multi-Stakeholder Blue Dot Network," U.S. International Development Finance Corporation (DFC), November 4, 2019, http://www.dfc.gov/media/opic-press-releases/launch-multistakeholder-blue-dot-network.

32. When initially set up, 70% of World Bank financing went to infrastructure. During 2015–2017, only 29% of World Bank support to ASEAN went to infrastructure. The figure for ADB was only slightly better at 39%. Drawn from chapter 5 in this volume by David Dollar.

33. For analysis of Sino-Japanese economic relations, including the prospects and challenges of cooperating in third countries, see Mireya Solís, "China, Japan, and the Art of Economic Statecraft" (Washington, DC: The Brookings Institution, February 2020), http://www.brookings.edu/wp-content/uploads/2020/02/FP_202002_china_japan_solis.pdf.

34. Drawn from chapter 2 in this volume by Lindsey Ford.

35. Drawn from chapter 5 and chapter 6 in this volume by David Dollar and Roland Rajah, respectively.

36. Drawn from chapter 5 in this volume by David Dollar.

37. Drawn from chapter 6 in this volume by Roland Rajah.

38. Joshua Kurlantzick, "Southeast Asia's Democratic Decline in the America First Era," Council on Foreign Relations, October 27, 2017, http://www.cfr.org/expert-brief/southeast-asias-democratic-decline-americafirst-era; and Huong Le Thu, "The Daunting State of Southeast Asian Democracy," Australian Strategic Policy Institute, May 8, 2018, http://www.aspistrategist.org.au/the-daunting-state-of-southeast-asiandemocracy/.

39. Sebastian Strangio, "In Southeast Asia, COVID-19 Slowly Tightens Its Grip," *The Diplomat*, September 18, 2020, https://thediplomat.com/2020/09/in-southeast-asia-covid-19-slowly-tightens-its-grip/.

40. Sang Minh Le, "Containing The Coronavirus (COVID-19): Lessons from Vietnam," World Bank Blogs, April 30, 2020, https://blogs.worldbank.org/health/containing-coronavirus-covid-19-lessons-vietnam?cid=SHR_BlogSiteShare_EN_EXT.

41. Trang (Mae) Nguyen and Edmund Malesky, "Reopening Vietnam: How the Country's Improving Governance Helped It Weather the COVID-19 Pandemic," The Brookings Institution, May 20, 2010, https://www.brookings.edu/blog/order-from-chaos/2020/05/20/reopening-vietnam-how-the-countrys-improving-governance-helped-it-weather-the-covid-19-pandemic/.

42. For analysis of China's potential impact governance trends in Southeast Asia, see Jonathan Stromseth and Hunter Marston, "Democracy at a Crossroads in Southeast Asia: Great Power Rivalry Meets Domestic Governance" (Washington, DC: The Brookings Institution, February 2018), http://www.brookings.edu/wpcontent/uploads/2019/02/FP_20190226_southeast_asia_stromseth_marston.pdf.

43. Drawn from chapter 8 in this volume by Ben Bland.

44. Drawn from chapter 9 in this volume by Thomas Pepinsky.

45. See Keith Bradsher, "With Covid-19 Under Control, China's Economy Surges Ahead," *New York Times*, October 19, 2020, https://www.nytimes.com/2020/10/18/business/china-economy-covid.html; and Issaku Harada, "ASEAN Becomes China's Top Trade Partner as Supply Chains Evolve," *Nikkei Asia*, July 15, 2020, https://asia.nikkei.com/Politics/International-relations/ASEAN-becomes-China-s-top-trade-partner-as-supply-chain-evolves.

46. For a discussion of the tremendous challenges facing the Chinese economy, such as fostering innovation and dealing with an aging population, see David Dollar, Yiping Huang, and Yang Yao, *China 2049: Economic Challenges of a Rising Global Power* (Washington, D.C.: Brookings Institution Press, 2020).

47. Danson Cheong, "COVID-19 Will Strain US-China Ties further, Pressure ASEAN to Pick Sides, Say Experts," *The Straits Times*, April 28, 2020, https://www.straitstimes.com/asia/east-asia/covid-19-will-strain-us-china-ties-further-pressure-asean-to-pick-sides.

48. Zacharias Szumer, "Coronavirus Spreads Anti-Chinese Feeling in Southeast Asia, but the Prejudice Goes Back Centuries," *South China Morning Post*, April 29, 2020, https://www.scmp.com/lifestyle/article/3081930/coronavirus-spreads-anti -chinese-feeling-southeast-asia-prejudice-goes.

49. Raul Dancel, "China's Feel-good Music Video on COVID-19 Help for Philippines Backfires, Sparks Anger Instead," *The Straits Times*, April 25, 2020, https://www.straitstimes.com/asia/se-asia/chinas-feel-good-music-video-on-covid -19-help-for-philippines-backfires-sparks-anger.

50. See Yudith Ho, "China Backs Indonesia to Become Vaccine Hub of Southeast Asia," Bloomberg, October 11, 2020, https://www.bloomberg.com/news/articles/ 2020-10-11/china-backs-indonesia-to-become-vaccine-hub-of-southeast-asia; and Jane Cai, "Vaccine Diplomacy: China, Indonesia Agree to Cooperate in Fight Against COVID-19," *South China Morning Post*, October 10, 2020, https://www. scmp.com/news/china/diplomacy/article/3104986/vaccine-diplomacy-china -indonesia-agree-cooperate-fight.

51. "Fact Sheet: United States-ASEAM Strategic Partnership" (U.S. Department of State, September 9, 2020), https://www.state.gov/united-states-asean-strategic -partnership/.

52. Yuen Yuen Ang, "When COVID-19 Meets Centralized, Personalized Power," *Nature Human Behavior* 4 (May 2020), 445-447, https://www.nature.com/articles/ s41562-020-0872-3.pdf.

53. Bonnie Bley, "A Middle-Power Moment," The Lowy Institute, August 23, 2019, http://www.lowyinstitute.org/the-interpreter/middle-power-moment.

2

The U.S. "Free and Open Indo-Pacific" Concept

Continuity and Change

LINDSEY FORD

INTRODUCTION

The surprise election of Donald Trump in 2016 raised significant questions about the future of U.S. engagement in the Indo-Pacific region. The Obama administration's "rebalance to Asia" was viewed in many quarters as an unfulfilled promise and there was little, if any, certainty about President Trump's own foreign policy priorities.

The Trump administration moved quickly to roll out a new "Free and Open Indo-Pacific" (FOIP) strategy in advance of President Trump's first visit to the region.[1] However, the administration's implementation of this strategy has been inconsistent. The positive and relatively conventional aspects of its Indo-Pacific strategy have been overshadowed and undermined by broader muscle movements in U.S. foreign policy, including the downward spiral in U.S.-China relations and the president's erratic instincts on alliance policy and international trade. The result has been a frequent disconnect between the rhetoric and reality of the administration's Indo-Pacific narrative, making it more challenging to rally support for U.S. initiatives as well as to send clear signals to adversaries.

This chapter explores the key themes and drivers of the Trump administration's Indo-Pacific strategy, outlining areas of consistency and change from previous U.S. administrations. It also evaluates implementation of the administration's strategy, arguing that tensions between the Indo-Pacific narrative and the administration's more confrontational foreign policy instincts have frequently undermined U.S. goals. Finally, this chapter looks forward, addressing opportunities for the United States to better align its Indo-Pacific initiatives with partners in Australia and Southeast Asia.

FROM THE REBALANCE TO THE FREE AND OPEN INDO-PACIFIC

After early uncertainty about whether the U.S. "rebalance to Asia" would endure after the 2016 presidential election, the Trump administration moved quickly to outline its own FOIP concept in late 2017. The first articulation of the administration's new concept was previewed by then Secretary of State Rex Tillerson in a speech at the Center for Strategic and International Studies.[2]

The initial rollout of the Indo-Pacific concept appeared less notable for what was new than what had remained the same. The most cited elements of the administration's new policy were the move to reframe the scope of U.S. strategy, by centering U.S. interests within a broader Indo-Pacific region, and to refocus multilateral cooperation around large regional democracies, highlighted by the administration's emphasis on a U.S.-Japan-Australia-India quadrilateral dialogue (known as "the Quad"). Yet both of these initiatives drew on ideas first endorsed by the George W. Bush and Barack Obama administrations.[3] Beyond "the Quad" and "the Indo-Pacific," the administration's rhetorical emphasis on regional security networks and shared principles were consistent with long-standing U.S. policy in the region. At the outset, the administration's Indo-Pacific strategy therefore suggested less a major rewrite of U.S. policy than a more traditional shift in emphasis between Democratic and Republican administrations.

The rollout of several strategic documents, including the U.S. National Security Strategy and the National Defense Strategy, soon made clear that despite many areas of continuity, more fundamental shifts were underway in U.S. foreign policy. The challenge for the Trump administration has been to reconcile these continuities and discontinuities within its approach to the Indo-Pacific.

America and the Indo-Pacific: Steady Interests and Shifting Threats

The most obvious area of consistency between the Trump administration's strategy and those of earlier U.S. administrations is its stated aim: "a free and open Indo-Pacific ... where sovereign and independent nations, with diverse cultures and many different dreams, can all prosper side-by-side, and thrive in freedom and in peace."[4] While aspirational, this statement reflects the relatively consistent way the United States has defined its interests in the Pacific over many years. As Michael Green argues, the central impulse of American strategy in the Pacific has been to ensure "the Pacific Ocean remains a conduit for American ideas and goods to flow westward, and not for threats to flow eastward toward the homeland."[5] In support of this interest, the United States has long made it a priority to protect the openness of Pacific sea lanes (and more recently, the "global commons"), promote a liberal political and economic order in the region, and maintain a robust military presence to deter instability and conflict.

U.S. foreign policy has also long been premised on the notion that maintaining a "free and open" Pacific requires the United States to prevent the rise of a regional power that could restrict U.S. access or establish a more insular regional order inimical to U.S. interests. It is this objective that serves as a departure point for the Trump administration's new strategy. Until relatively recently, there was little indication that U.S. policymakers saw an existential threat to American interests in the Indo-Pacific. Hilary Clinton's 2011 Foreign Policy article, "America's Pacific Century," painted a relatively optimistic view of the Asian region, focused on its geopolitical influence, economic dynamism, and movement toward "a more mature security and economic architecture." The focus of the U.S. rebalance strategy was to enhance U.S. influence and consolidate positive momentum in a region of increasing geostrategic importance.

By contrast, the Trump administration's 2017 U.S. National Security Strategy provides a notably different threat assessment. It describes a "geopolitical competition between free and repressive visions of world order" underway in the Indo-Pacific, with China seeking to "challenge American power, influence, and interests ... [and] erode American security and prosperity."[6] This document represented the U.S. government's first attempt to openly wrestle with a new reality: For the first time in decades, the United States was contending with a regional competitor with the necessary economic and military power to challenge some of its most vital interests.

New Trends in American Foreign Policy

Flowing from this altered threat assessment, the Trump administration's strategy re-envisions the *ways* in which the United States should pursue its aims. Under the banner of President Trump's "America First" vision, U.S. foreign policy has been re-centered around the idea of global "competition." Although President Trump's America First message has not been embraced across the U.S. electorate, the idea that America needs to compete and restore U.S. "advantages in key areas" has gained bipartisan traction.[7] The root causes of this shift precede the president's election. Two factors—one domestic and one foreign—help explain the current shift in U.S. foreign policy.

For several decades, U.S. leaders have enjoyed relatively bipartisan support for a liberal internationalist foreign policy, one rooted in the belief that removing interstate barriers to trade and commerce, promoting good governance and democratization, and enmeshing states into rules-based international institutions would advance American interests. Two decades of declining economic and military dominance, lengthy overseas military interventions, and rising inequality have undermined support for this approach.

President Trump's belief that liberal internationalism has failed in rather serious ways is one that now resonates with many parts of the American public. Americans have not given up on global engagement; this is clear from repeated surveys.[8] There is, however, bipartisan momentum behind the idea that America should do more to alter the terms of international leadership. On the economic front, politicians on both the right and left have become more skeptical of the relative costs and benefits of U.S. trade agreements, an issue that has found particular resonance in the decade following the 2008–2009 Great Recession. Although most Americans still endorse free trade in principle, 2017 Gallup polls showed widespread support for President Trump's commitment to renegotiate existing U.S. agreements.[9] Similarly, while support for U.S. alliances is stronger than ever, the president's rhetoric about the need for allies to "pay their fair share" has found support in many quarters. One recent poll indicated nearly 50% of the public believed that the United States should not have to honor its commitments to NATO if allies did not increase their defense spending.[10]

Beyond changes in U.S. domestic politics, the idea of a more competitive U.S. foreign policy is also a response to the changing nature of U.S.-China relations. The Trump administration's National Security Strategy made clear that the administration would no longer adhere to the dual-track approach of engagement and hedging that had characterized U.S.-China relations for over 30 years, instead doubling down on "strategic competition" with Beijing. In part, this shift reflects changes in the structural underpinnings of the U.S.-China relationship. Beijing's rapid accrual of economic, military, geopolitical, and technological power has created new domains of competition with Washington, expanding mutual friction points into areas such as emerging technologies and global governance. The result, as Evan Medeiros has argued, is that "primacy of competition has become a core feature of the US-China relationship."[11]

However, the bipartisan pessimism about U.S.-China relations that now pervades U.S. policymaking is driven less by the reality of China's rise than by frustration over how China has chosen to use its increased power. Over the past few years, Chinese leaders have more aggressively wielded tools including military operations in the South and East China Seas, domestic political influence campaigns, and economic boycott threats to coerce other nations and limit U.S. influence. U.S. concerns about these actions have grown since Xi Jinping took the helm in China. Presidents Obama and Xi Jinping famously discussed a "new model" for U.S.-China ties in their 2013 Sunnylands Summit, but the tension between Washington and Beijing became more obvious throughout President Obama's second term. Even as the Obama administration continued to seek new diplomatic accords to manage areas of disagreement, other actions, such as pressing China on state-sponsored cyber-espionage and initiating new U.S. Freedom of Navigation operations in the South China Sea, presaged a downward trend in the bilateral relationship.[12]

RECONCILING COMPETITION AND THE FREE AND OPEN INDO-PACIFIC

At first glance, the basic building blocks of the Trump administration's Free and Open Indo-Pacific strategy appear conventional. They are consistent with long-standing principles of U.S. engagement in the Pacific—building collective security through a network of regional allies and partners, promoting economic prosperity, and encouraging good governance and shared principles. Yet the liberal international vision these principles support is fundamentally misaligned with the president's own view of the world and incongruent with the administration's America First message. The administration has attempted to reconcile this misalignment by orienting both its Indo-Pacific strategy and the America First message around the idea of competition. Pursuing a more competitive strategy need not be incompatible with traditional tenets of U.S. leadership. In fact, China's aggressive behavior toward its neighbors creates new opportunities, and a greater need, to defend these long-standing principles and rally a stronger collective response to Beijing's destabilizing behavior. But in execution, the president's narrow America First narrative alters the perceived aims of this competition, often undermining the stated objectives of the administration's Indo-Pacific initiatives. This section explores some of these tensions in the Trump administration's Indo-Pacific strategy.

Reorienting Alliances and Partnerships

The U.S. alliance and partnership network has been the centerpiece of American strategy in Asia since World War II, and the principal means through which the United States promotes collective security in the Indo-Pacific. For the past two administrations, the United States has worked to expand this network beyond its traditional emphasis on Northeast Asia, increasingly focusing on new U.S. partnerships in Southeast and South Asia. The Trump administration's pointed move to embrace an "Indo-Pacific" construct builds on this trend, reflecting not only American efforts to more fully incorporate India into the East Asian strategic environment, but also to recognize the connectivity between the Indian and Pacific oceans.

One notable development under the Trump administration has been its focus on expanding U.S. engagement with smaller nations in the Indian Ocean and Pacific Islands regions. In South Asia, the administration has worked to tighten relationships with countries such as Nepal and Sri Lanka, offering new high-level dialogues and assistance that includes $500 million toward infrastructure development in Nepal and a high-endurance Coast Guard cutter for Sri Lanka.[13] In Southeast Asia, the administration has prioritized engagement in the Mekong region, including a new Japan-U.S. Mekong Power Partnership and additional funding to counter transnational crime and trafficking.[14] The administration has also offered new forms of technical assistance and advice to countries such as Myanmar that have enabled them to improve the terms of their infrastructure loans with Beijing. Another positive development has been the revitalization of U.S. relationships in the Pacific Islands region, which had long been a relatively peripheral element of U.S. regional engagement.

Beyond enhancing bilateral ties, the Trump administration has also continued earlier administrations' efforts to promote stronger "minilateral" networks between U.S. partners. A growing sense of shared concern about Chinese influence has helped propel new momentum for these dialogues in the past few years, facilitating combined naval operations in the South China Sea, collaboration on debt transparency and infrastructure standard setting, and even digital connectivity initiatives. Much attention has been given to the administration's efforts to revitalize the Quadrilateral Dialogue between the United States, Australia, India, and Japan, but the Trump administration has also engaged partners through additional multilateral initiatives. These include agreements with Australia, India, Japan, Singapore, and Taiwan to coordinate development assistance in third-party countries; increased support for the Lower Mekong Initiative; and a new collaboration between the United States, Australia, and Papua New Guinea to modernize the Lombrum naval base.

Despite these positive developments, the broader trend line for U.S. alliances and partnerships has been far more negative under the Trump administration. One of the principal weaknesses of the administration's approach is that it has often created the perception that Washington's interests are misaligned with those of its friends. As noted above, many U.S. allies and partners quietly share the administration's concerns about Chinese influence and its desire to prevent Chinese hegemony in the region.[15] But this is not their only concern. The president's absence from multilateral venues such as the East Asia Summit, and retreat from cooperation on issues that matter deeply to regional partners, such as climate change, suggests a lack of interest in the region's priorities. This has led partners to vocally express frustration with a U.S strategy that at times appears less focused on the ambitions and security interests of America's friends than on improving the U.S. position vis-à-vis Beijing.[16]

The Trump administration's approach has also exposed fault lines between the United States and its partners over their tolerance for open confrontation with Beijing. In general, U.S. partners envision an Indo-Pacific order that tends to accommodate a greater degree of coexistence, and more limited confrontation, with Beijing than Washington might prefer. In practice, this means U.S. allies and partners are often willing to entertain cooperation in areas where Washington is not, such as Japan's willingness to cooperate with China's Belt and Road Initiative (BRI),[17] or Singapore's recent decision to sign a new bilateral Singapore-China defense agreement.[18] At times, it also limits their willingness to endorse security initiatives likely to spark friction with Beijing.

To some degree, misalignments between Washington and its regional partners are not new or surprising. They reflect differences in the degree to which countries see their economic and political futures as reliant upon productive ties with Beijing. Yet rather than closing these gaps, the Trump administration has often exacerbated them, by creating the impression that ties with China may come at the cost of relations with the United States.

Regional frustration over the confrontational tone of the administration's narrative on 5G technology and "debt trap diplomacy" is often apparent. Regional leaders have complained that Washington's calls to decouple with Beijing ignore the constraints facing smaller partners, asking U.S. allies to shoulder significant economic and political risk with little upside gain and few available alternatives. As former Malaysian Prime Minister Mohammed Mahathir bluntly argued: "We cannot afford to build these very expensive railway lines. Whether we like it or not, we have to go to the Chinese."[19] Nations such as Singapore have expressed concern that U.S.-China strategic rivalry is constraining their strategic space rather than expanding it, making it more difficult for countries to balance between the superpowers.[20] The result is that some partners have become increasingly wary of *both* Washington and Beijing, with even close allies and partners openly advocating for a more autonomous foreign policy path.

Promoting Shared Principles

Much like the Obama administration, the Trump administration's Indo-Pacific strategy emphasizes the importance of certain principles of inter-state relations, including respect for state sovereignty and independence; free and fair trade; peaceful resolution of disputes; and respect for international rules, including freedom of navigation and overflight. It has offered support for these principles on various fronts, including expanding U.S. Freedom of Navigation operations in contested areas of the South China Sea, increasing maritime capacity-building support for Southeast Asian and Pacific Island nations, working alongside G-20 leaders to promote new Principles for Quality Infrastructure Investment, and announcing a new $400 million Indo-Pacific Transparency Initiative. These initiatives are consistent with a long-standing U.S. emphasis on promoting shared rules of the road and norms of behavior in the Indo-Pacific. The administration has also tightened its coordination with allies and partners on this front, developing initiatives such as the Blue Dot Network, which will work with Japan, Australia, and others to promote high standards in infrastructure development.

Once again, however, the administration's own messaging has at times worked at cross-purposes with its goals. One of the more notable shifts in U.S. messaging under the Trump administration has been its emphasis on "reciprocity" as a core principle of U.S. engagement. In his October 2018 speech at the Hudson Institute, Vice President Mike Pence argued the United States seeks a relationship with China "grounded in fairness, reciprocity, and respect for sovereignty."[21] Much of the administration's emphasis on "reciprocity" is rooted in frustration over Chinese economic policies, especially Beijing's use of state subsidies, technology theft, and data localization laws to create an unfair playing field for U.S. companies. These are concerns that resonate with U.S. partners both in and outside the region.

However, the administration has not only targeted Beijing with its reciprocity agenda. Instead, the president has extended his focus to partners across the Indo-Pacific region, repeatedly decrying the unfairness of U.S. alliance relationships. On the economic front, the administration has pressured countries to reduce their trade deficits with the United States, pushed South Korea to update the Korea-U.S. Free Trade agreement, and engaged in a back-and-forth tariff dispute with India.[22] The administration has pressed allies on the security front as well, frequently criticizing the cost of U.S. forces in the Pacific and demanding dramatic increases in host nation support for U.S. forces in South Korea and Japan.[23]

The administration's concerns about market access problems and inequal burden-sharing are not without merit and certainly not unprecedented. Previous U.S. administrations often engaged their foreign counterparts in discussions about these issues.[24] However, these discussions were rooted in the belief that U.S. alliances generated positive sum gains for both the United States and its partners. President Trump's rhetoric instead suggests a one-way relationship in which U.S. alliances are a net negative that provide "virtually nothing" to Washington in return.[25] By ignoring the ways in which America's Asian allies have allowed the United States to pursue its regional interests at a lower relative cost, the president's rhetoric suggests the United States is less motivated by principles of fairness and mutual benefit than by the pursuit of unilateral gains—even at the expense of its friends.

Equally problematic is the fact that the administration's embrace of regional principles often appears haphazard and inconsistent. The administration has insistently pursued denuclearization of the Korean Peninsula and emphasized its commitment to global counter-proliferation efforts.[26] Yet the president has also deployed new low-yield nuclear weapons and openly mused that U.S. allies should pursue nuclear programs of their own.[27] Despite the administration's frequent advocacy for democracy and human rights, President Trump referred to democracy protests in Hong Kong as "a complicating factor" in achieving his goal of a trade deal with Beijing.[28] Similarly, the president has repeatedly lavished praise on regional leaders such as Kim Jong Un and Rodrigo Duterte, even congratulating the latter for doing an "unbelievable job" in a drug war that has involved thousands of reported extrajudicial killings.[29] The legitimacy of American leadership has long resided in its willingness to endorse a consistent set of rules and principles that apply to all nations, both large and small. The inconsistency between the administration's words and deeds undermines this goal.[30]

Promoting Prosperity

The Trump administration's economic strategy has been perhaps the most contentious, and underdeveloped, element of its Indo-Pacific strategy. As outlined by Secretary of State Mike Pompeo, the Trump administration's economic strategy is centered around promoting "open investment environments, transparent agreements between nations, and improved connectivity."[31] Unlike the Obama administration, which made negotiating the Trans-Pacific Partnership (TPP) trade agreement the centerpiece of its regional economic strategy, the Trump administration has instead emphasized its desire to strengthen private-sector business and investment ties, and promote entrepreneurship. In part, this emphasis reflects the administration's own domestic economic agenda, but it also aims to draw a contrast with China's state-driven development model, which it has widely criticized as facilitating corruption, poor environmental and labor standards, and unsustainable levels of debt.

In response to early critiques that U.S. strategy lacked a positive economic agenda, the Trump administration articulated three priorities for its regional economic plan: energy security, infrastructure development, and digital connectivity. In support of these goals, the administration rolled out a series of new initiatives, including a trilateral Memorandum of Understanding on infrastructure development with Japan and Australia; ASIA Edge, a new initiative to strengthen regional energy security; and a U.S.-Association of Southeast Asian Nations (ASEAN) Smart Cities partnership to support digital connectivity in Southeast Asia. The administration has also pursued select regional bilateral trade agreements, including an update to the Korea-U.S. Free Trade Agreement as well as a limited trade agreement with Japan.

Much like the other elements of its strategy, the Trump administration's economic agenda has been muddled. On the one hand, the administration's desire to boost private-sector ties and strengthen energy security and digital cooperation plays to U.S. strengths. Congressional passage of the Better Utilization of Investment Leading to Development (BUILD) Act and the establishment of the new U.S. International Development Finance Corporation complements this work by incentivizing a greater private-sector role within the U.S. development agenda. All of these efforts are consistent with what has been a hallmark American approach to Indo-

Pacific development for decades: identifying shared economic priorities that drive growth both at home *and* abroad.

Despite these positive steps, the affirmative elements of the administration's agenda pale in comparison to the more insular aspects of its economic strategy. What has been most damaging on the economic front is the administration's inability to develop a positive narrative on international trade. The most high-profile aspect of the administration's trade agenda has been a negative one for many Asian partners: the wide-ranging tariffs the United States has levied in the trade war between Washington and Beijing. The TPP, which the Trump administration jettisoned early on, signaled America's intent to promote high-standard free trade across the region. The Trump administration's approach, by contrast, has been more divisive. Some countries, such as Vietnam and Bangladesh, have benefited from the redirection of global supply chains away from Beijing.[32] Other U.S. partners, including South Korea, Singapore, and Japan, have experienced slowing economic growth, and Asian Development Bank forecasts suggest worsening economic trends for the region as a whole.[33]

Rather than producing broad-based prosperity, a longtime U.S. goal, the Trump administration's approach appears to create discrete winners and losers. The administration's decision to pursue bilateral instead of multilateral trade agreements reinforces this perception. The agreements the administration has secured thus far have done little to provide a foundation for regionwide growth. The administration's most successful negotiations to date—those with Japan and South Korea—secured only moderate changes to the status quo. Meanwhile, its efforts to seek comprehensive deals with China and India both stalled, forcing the administration to settle for a narrow "Phase One" deal with the Chinese and the promise of further talks with India. The absence of a more credible and robust economic strategy has only reinforced China's narrative that the United States lacks the capacity or will to restore the regional economic architecture it once built.

ASSESSING U.S. STRATEGY

The Trump administration's Indo-Pacific strategy offers important points of both continuity and change. First, it endorses, at least rhetorically, the enduring nature of America's interests in the Indo-Pacific region. Second, it openly acknowledges the need for a much more profound reckoning with the ways in which China's rise is reshaping the Indo-Pacific order.

Yet where the administration's implementation of its strategy misses the mark so drastically is its inability to reconcile these two ideas in practice. The administration's confrontational narrative and the markedly unilateral ambitions of its America First vision extend beyond China to U.S. allies and partners, which has unmoored American strategy from its grounding in the pursuit of shared interests. Similarly, the administration's inability to address the China challenge in a way that doesn't undermine long-standing tenets of American leadership—such as strengthening U.S. alliances, advancing economic openness, and supporting liberal values— has been deeply problematic.

The inconsistencies between the administration's "free and open" narrative and its actions abound—in deploying tariffs on close partners, in the president's relatively muted support for democratic protesters in Hong Kong, and in berating close allies over host nation support for U.S. forces. These inconsistencies have undermined U.S. strategy on various fronts:

■ **Fears about American reliability are fueling a search for additional strategic options.** Repeated polls have shown that the U.S. partners express a lack of trust in President Trump to "do the right thing" when it comes to global affairs.[34] This is fueling fears of both abandonment and entrapment among some U.S. allies. The result is not a rush to bandwagon with Beijing, but rather increasing discussions of additional options such as "strategic autonomy" or "middle-power diplomacy." In short, many Asian countries are looking for a back-up plan that depends less on either Washington or Beijing.

■ **Zero-sum rhetoric complicates coalition-building efforts.** The perception that U.S. strategy is more focused on containing China than on providing collective goods has dampened enthusiasm for the Trump administration's Indo-Pacific strategy. Close partners such as South Korea and ASEAN have been reluctant to fully endorse the Free and Open Indo-Pacific concept or be seen as aligning too closely with FOIP-branded initiatives. The narrow and defensive posture of the administration's strategy also limits opportunities for America to shape a wider regional agenda and incentivize collective action on issues ranging from climate change to global health and education.

■ **U.S. unilateralism reinforces Chinese efforts to reshape regional order.** Beijing has long decried U.S. security alliances and principles as Cold War relics ill-suited to the contemporary Asian security environment. It has instead called for a "new Asian security concept" more closely aligned with Beijing's preferences.[35] President Trump's frequent denigration of U.S. alliances and his willingness to undermine regional principles only reinforces Beijing's messaging, accelerating its efforts to weaken alliance networks and reshape a new Asian security architecture.

RECOMMENDATIONS AND OPPORTUNITIES FOR TRILATERAL COORDINATION

The evident tensions between the Trump administration's free and open Indo-Pacific narrative and the president's focus on a competitive foreign policy are equally apparent in U.S. relationships with partners in Australia and ASEAN. On the one hand, the administration's desire to compete with Beijing has opened new avenues of cooperation between the United States and partners in Southeast Asia. Shared concerns about China's political and economic influence have deepened coordination between Canberra and Washington on issues ranging from 5G technologies to infrastructure and development assistance. Similarly, the Trump administration's renewed attention to Mekong region states has broadened U.S. engagement in Southeast Asia to a wider range of partners.

Yet at the same time, the Trump administration's approach has exposed new fault lines in these relationships. Even as the Australian government has pursued a tougher line toward Beijing, Australian policymakers and experts have also been candid that Canberra's interests and policies will not fully align with Washington's preferences.[36] ASEAN states have similarly published their own "ASEAN Outlook on the Indo-Pacific" in an effort to stake out an independent voice on regional security dynamics.[37] President Trump's unwillingness to more fully consider his partners' interests—highlighted by a tense introductory phone call with former Australian leader Malcolm Turnbull as well as the president's repeated absence from U.S.-ASEAN leaders' meetings—only deepens these divides.

These fault lines undoubtedly create challenges for the U.S. policymakers and their counterparts, but they do not pose insurmountable obstacles to closer coordination. The shared values and interests between the United States and its partners continue to vastly outweigh any differences. Going forward, the three partners should identify opportunities for closer coordination using a simple, three-part rubric: *exchange, coordinate, collaborate.* Under this approach, in areas where partners are likely to have misaligned interests or threat perceptions, they should focus on simple efforts to more transparently *exchange* information. In areas where there are elements of both agreement and disagreement, they should maximize commonalities by working to *coordinate* national-level initiatives. And finally, in areas where the partners have closely aligned interests, they should seek opportunities to *collaborate* on integrated policy initiatives.

A few examples of potential areas to for further trilateral engagement include:

▪ **Exchange candid assessments on China.** Washington and its partners are unlikely to fully reconcile their differences over how to approach Beijing in the near future. But this does not mean they should not engage in more open and candid exchanges about how each country is managing the areas of cooperation and competition in its relationship with China. This will become increasingly necessary as the domains of competition between Washington and Beijing grow. Washington needs to hear from its partners where their priorities may differ from its own, and why. Similarly, U.S. partners would benefit from a deeper understanding of U.S. policy, to help assuage combined concerns about abandonment and entrapment.

▪ **Coordinate on digital connectivity.** ASEAN has made it a priority to improve digital connectivity within Southeast Asia. The United States and Australia are both partners in this effort, and both countries participate in ASEAN's Smart Cities initiatives. While there may be differences between various countries regarding their preferred digital standards and norms, there are nonetheless opportunities for greater coordination. The United States and Australia could discuss with individual Southeast Asian states how to better align the assistance they provide through their Smart City initiatives and coordinate cyber capacity-building training and activities. As countries continue to debate international standards in the cyber and digital domains, ASEAN, Australia, and the United States might also consider a trilateral dialogue to discuss digital governance issues such as data privacy and cyber sovereignty.

■ **Collaborate on Mekong region development assistance.** The United States, Australia, and ASEAN are all engaging in the Mekong through different dialogue mechanisms. This proliferation of dialogues presents a coordination challenge for riparian states. All of the parties share an interest in facilitating more sustainable and transparent resource management that will prevent instability and poverty in Southeast Asia. Policymakers could explore opportunities to develop collaborative approaches by sharing country-level needs assessments, establishing trilateral development projects, and endorsing similar resource-management principles and standards.

CONCLUSION

In spite of early concerns that the Trump administration might walk away from the U.S. pivot to Asia, his administration's Indo-Pacific strategy confirms Asia's important place in American foreign policy. On some fronts, such as efforts to enhance ties with strong democratic partners like Japan and India, the administration's strategy reaffirms consistent, bipartisan priorities that have guided American engagement in Asia for decades. On others—principally, the administration's approach toward China and international trade—the Trump administration's approach is frequently dissonant with the positive-sum ambitions of its Indo-Pacific vision.

The principal weakness of the administration's approach on both of these issues is that by attempting to marry strategic competition with the nationalism of the president's America First vision, it has muddied the waters of U.S. strategy. The president's threat-centric, protectionist rhetoric implicitly suggests the United States has walked away from what has made American leadership so distinct: its emphasis on promoting collective goods rather than pursuing narrow, unilateral aims.

The administration's rhetoric has complicated efforts to build closer coordination with close U.S. partners in the region, creating unnecessary areas of friction in its relationships with close partners such as Australia and ASEAN. This approach only expands the opportunities for Beijing to exploit gaps between the United States and its allies and weaken regional security networks. Going forward, the United States and its partners should not shy away from a frank acknowledgment of areas of disagreement, but they must also work more aggressively to prevent these disagreements from undermining their collective interests. The United States, Australia, and ASEAN are aligned in a shared vision of a free and open Indo-Pacific. By focusing on the opportunities to build collective action in pursuit of this goal, they can maintain a positive agenda for multilateral cooperation.

Notes

1. "Indo-Pacific Strategy Report: Preparedness, Partnerships, And Promoting a Networked Region" (Washington, DC: U.S. Department of Defense, June 1, 2019), 4, https://media.defense.gov/2019/Jul/01/2002152311/-1/-1/1/DEPARTMENT-OF -DEFENSE-INDO-PACIFIC-STRATEGY-REPORT-2019.PDF.

2. Rex Tillerson, "Defining Our Relationship with India for the Next Century" (speech, Center for Strategic and International Studies, Washington, DC, October 18, 2017), https://www.csis.org/analysis/defining-our-relationship-india-next -century-address-us-secretary-state-rex-tillerson.

3. The first quadrilateral meeting between Australia, India, Japan, and the United States occurred on the margins of the ASEAN Regional Forum in May 2007 under the George W. Bush administration. Although the United States did not formally adopt the "Indo-Pacific" terminology into its strategic documents until the Trump administration, Obama administration officials frequently deployed the term in an effort to emphasize the connectivity between the Indian and Pacific Oceans. For more, see Tanvi Madan, "The Rise, Fall, And Rebirth Of The 'Quad,'" War on the Rocks, November 16, 2017, https://warontherocks.com/2017/11/rise-fall -rebirth-quad/; Rory Medcalf, "The Indo-Pacific: What's in a Name?," *The American Interest*, October 10, 2013, https://www.the-american-interest.com/2013/10/10/the -indo-pacific-whats-in-a-name/.

4. Donald Trump, "Remarks by President Trump at the APEC CEO Summit."

5. Michael J. Green, *By More Than Providence* (New York: Columbia University Press, 2019), 5.

6. "National Security Strategy of the United States of America" (Washington, DC: The White House, December 2017), https://www.whitehouse.gov/wp-content/ uploads/2017/12/NSS-Final-12-18-2017-0905-2.pdf.

7. Ibid, page 12.

8. Dina Smeltz et al., "America Engaged" (Chicago: The Chicago Council on Global Affairs, October 2, 2018), https://www.thechicagocouncil.org/publication/ lcc/america-engaged.

9. Lydia Saad, "Americans' Views on Trade in the Trump Era," Gallup, October

25, 2019, https://news.gallup.com/opinion/gallup/267770/americans-views-trade
-trump-era.aspx.

10. David Brennan, "Half of Americans Don't Want to Defend NATO Allies If
Spending Commitments Don't Increase," *Newsweek*, July 19, 2018, https://www.
newsweek.com/half-americans-dont-want-defend-nato-allies-if-spending-com
mitments-dont-1032117.

11. Evan S. Medeiros, "The Changing Fundamentals of U.S.-China Relations,"
Washington Quarterly, 42, no. 3 (July 2019): 93-119, https://www.researchgate.net/
publication/336446277_The_Changing_Fundamentals_of_US-China_Relations.

12. Michael S. Schmidt and David E. Sanger, "5 in China Army Face U.S. Charges
of Cyberattacks," *The New York Times*, May 19, 2014, https://www.nytimes.com/
2014/05/20/us/us-to-charge-chinese-workers-with-cyberspying.html; Ankit Panda,
"After Months of Waiting, US Finally Begins Freedom of Navigation Patrols Near
China's Man-Made Islands," *The Diplomat*, October 27, 2015, https://thediplomat.
com/2015/10/after-months-of-waiting-us-finally-begins-freedom-of-navigation
-patrols-near-chinas-man-made-islands/.

13. Heather Nauert, "U.S. and Nepal Sign $500 Million Compact," U.S.
Department of State, September 14, 2017, https://www.state.gov/u-s-and-nepal-sign
-500-million-compact/; Gabriel Dominguez, "Ex-US Coast Guard Cutter Arrives in
Sri Lanka," Jane's Defence Weekly, May 13, 2019, https://www.janes.com/article/
88474/ex-us-coast-guard-cutter-arrives-in-sri-lanka.

14. "Strengthening the U.S.-Mekong Partnership (Fact Sheet)," U.S. Department
of State, August 2, 2019, https://www.state.gov/strengthening-the-u-s-mekong
-partnership/.

15. "The State of Southeast Asia: 2020 Survey Report" (Singapore: ISEAS-Yusof
Ishak Institute, January 16, 2020), https://www.iseas.edu.sg/images/pdf/TheStateof
SEASurveyReport_2020.pdf.

16. Uri Friedman, "America is Alone in its Cold War with China," *The Atlantic*,
February 17, 2020, https://www.theatlantic.com/politics/archive/2020/02/us-china
-allies-competition/606637/.

17. Junnosuke Kobara and Oki Nagai, "China and Japan Move Closer to Coop-
erating on Belt and Road," *Nikkei Asia*, August 3, 2018, https://asia.nikkei.com/
Politics/International-relations/China-and-Japan-move-closer-to-cooperating-on
-Belt-and-Road.

18. "Fact Sheet: Enhanced Agreement on Defence Exchanges and Security
Cooperation (ADESC)," Ministry of Defence and the Singapore Armed Forces,
October 21, 2019, https://www.mindef.gov.sg/web/portal/mindef/news-and-events/
latest-releases/article-detail/2019/October/20oct19_fs.

19. Marrian Zhou, "Mahathir: 'We Have to Go to the Chinese' for Infrastructure,"
Nikkei Asia, September 27, 2019, https://asia.nikkei.com/Politics/International
-relations/Mahathir-We-have-to-go-to-the-Chinese-for-infrastructure.

20. Lee Hsien Loong, "Keynote address at the Shangri-La Dialogue Opening
Dinner" (speech, Singapore, May 31, 2019), https://www.pmo.gov.sg/Newsroom/
PM-Lee-Hsien-Loong-at-the-IISS-Shangri-La-Dialogue-2019.

21. Mike Pence, "Vice President Pence's Remarks on the Administration's Policy

Toward China" (speech, Washington, DC, October 4, 2018), https://www.hudson.org/events/1610-vice-president-mike-pence-s-remarks-on-the-administration-s-policy-towards-china102018.

22. Alexia Fernández Campbell, "Trump's New Trade Deal with South Korea, Explained," Vox, September 24, 2018, https://www.vox.com/2018/9/24/17883506/trump-korea-trade-deal-korus; Vindu Goel, "India Raises Tariffs, Escalating Trade Fight With Trump," *The New York Times*, June 15, 2019, https://www.nytimes.com/2019/06/15/business/india-tariffs-trade-trump.html.

23. Diana Stancy Correll, "Demanding South Korea Pay More for US Presence Drives Wedge between Allies, House Leaders Say," *Military Times*, December 3, 2019, https://www.militarytimes.com/news/your-military/2019/12/03/demanding-south-korea-exponentially-increase-payments-to-keep-us-troops-there-will-drive-needless-wedge-between-us-and-our-allies-say-house-leaders/.

24. Hana Kusumoto, "U.S., Japan Sign New Five-Year 'Host Nation Support' Agreement," *Star and Stripes*, January 21, 2011, https://www.stripes.com/news/pacific/japan/u-s-japan-sign-new-five-year-host-nation-support-agreement-1.132428.

25. William Gallo, "In South Korea, a Small But Notable Backlash Against Trump," Voice of America, August 20, 2019, https://www.voanews.com/east-asia-pacific/south-korea-small-notable-backlash-against-trump.

26. "Fact Sheet: President Donald J. Trump is Committed to Countering the Proliferation of Chemical, Biological, and Nuclear Weapons," The White House, September 26, 2018, https://www.whitehouse.gov/briefings-statements/president-donald-j-trump-committed-countering-proliferation-chemical-biological-nuclear-weapons/.

27. "Full Rush Transcript: Donald Trump, CNN Milwaukee Republican Presidential Town Hall," CNN Press Room, March 29, 2016, https://cnnpressroom.blogs.cnn.com/2016/03/29/full-rush-transcript-donald-trump-cnn-milwaukee-republican-presidential-town-hall/.

28. Scott Horsley, "President Trump Waffles On Hong Kong Democracy Bill Amid China Trade Talks," NPR, November 22, 2019, https://www.npr.org/2019/11/22/781972199/president-trump-waffles-on-hong-kong-democracy-bill.

29. Joshua Berlinger and Elise Labott, "Trump Praises Duterte's Deadly Drug War in Leaked Transcript," CNN, May 24, 2017, https://www.cnn.com/2017/05/24/politics/donald-trump-rodrigo-duterte-phone-call-transcript/index.html.

30. Keith Johnson, "How Trump May Finally Kill the WTO," *Foreign Policy*, December 9, 2019, https://foreignpolicy.com/2019/12/09/trump-may-kill-wto-finally-appellate-body-world-trade-organization/.

31. Mike Pompeo, "America's Indo-Pacific Economic Vision" (speech, Washington, DC, July 30, 2018), https://www.state.gov/remarks-on-americas-indo-pacific-economic-vision/.

32. Robin Harding, "Asia's Emerging Economies Are Winning US-China Trade War," *Financial Times*, September 25, 2019, https://www.ft.com/content/b01d048c-df59-11e9-9743-db5a370481bc.

33. Ibid.

34. Richard Wike et al., "Trump Ratings Remain Low Around Globe, While Views of U.S. Stay Mostly Favorable," Pew Research Center, January 8, 2020, https:/ /www.pewresearch.org/global/2020/01/08/trump-ratings-remain-low-around -globe-while-views-of-u-s-stay-mostly-favorable/.

35. Xi Jinping, "New Asian Security Concept For New Progress in Security Cooperation" (speech, Shanghai, May 21, 2014), https://www.fmprc.gov.cn/mfa_eng /zxxx_662805/t1159951.shtml.

36. Charles Edel and John Lee, "The Future of US-Australia Alliance In an Era of Great Power Competition" (Sydney: United States Studies Centre, 2019), https:// united-states-studies-centre.s3.amazonaws.com/uploads/b4d/163/833/b4d163833 df2788a1f901cec358849bd31381eec/The-future-of-the-US-Australia-alliance-in-an -era-of-great-power-competition.pdf.

37. ASEAN Outlook on the Indo-Pacific," Association of Southeast Asian Nations, June 23, 2019, https://asean.org/asean-outlook-indo-pacific/.

3

At a Strategic Crossroads

ASEAN Centrality amid Sino-American Rivalry in the Indo-Pacific

RICHARD JAVAD HEYDARIAN

INTRODUCTION: A CHINESE WORLD ORDER?

In his 2014 book *World Order*, Henry Kissinger warns that an existing order—a set of commonly accepted rules, both formal and codified, which undergird inter-state relations—atrophies when there is "either a re-definition of legitimacy or a significant shift in the balance of power."[1] In the past decade, China's rise and its attendant foreign policy assertiveness have represented both a rapid shift in the balance of power and a direct assault on the legitimacy of the U.S.-led liberal international order in the Indo-Pacific mega-region.[2] And this should come as no surprise.

Reflecting on the future of the region's security architecture, the late Singaporean Prime Minister Lee Kuan Yew cautioned: "The size of China's displacement of the world balance is such that the world must find a new balance. It is not possible to pretend that this is just another big player. This is the biggest player in the history of the world."[3] Beyond just a tactical "balance-of-power" readjustment, Lee warned, China's reemergence as a great power portends a systemic shock to the post–World War II international system.[4]

More subtly, China has tried to challenge the existing order through the introduction of ambitious multilateral economic initiatives, first the Asian Infrastructure Investment Bank (AIIB) and, more notably later, the Belt and Road Initiative (BRI). On the most fundamental level, these initiatives seek to reorient both the hard and soft infrastructure of the Eurasian landmass and rimlands with Chinese characteristics, as more nations not only welcome large-scale Chinese loans and infrastructure investments, but also adopt Chinese techno-industrial standards and modes of governance. Without a doubt, bureaucratic politics, corporate and local government lobbying,[5] and domestic developmental imperatives (especially the desperate drive to uplift conditions in China's landlocked and ethnically mixed regions) are some of the endogenous drivers behind the BRI.[6] But as the veteran European diplomat Bruno Maçães pithily put it, the BRI and related projects are about creating a new Chinese-dominated order, first regionally but ultimately globally.[7] (Although, some studies show that Beijing is so far primarily interested in consolidating existing trade linkages, rather than superimposing its vision onto the global geopolitical canvass.[8])

No wonder then, that China's challenge to the existing order is far from confined to the realm of investments and trade. Relishing its expanding military muscle, China has upped the ante in the past decade. Over a span of only eighteen months between 2013 and 2015, China reclaimed—on an unprecedented scale and through once-unimaginable geoengineering—as much as 1,170 hectares (2,900 acres) across the disputed Spratly Islands. These are among the biggest artificial islands in the middle of high seas, with a sprawling network of advanced military and civilian facilities in the heart of one of the world's most important sea lines of communication. In recent years, China has effectively built the foundation of an air defense identification zone in a strategic chokepoint, as it boasts multiple artificial islands—namely the Fiery Cross, Mischief, and Subi reefs—that host advanced military assets as well as three-kilometer-long airstrips capable of accomodating large military aircraft. This allows Beijing to project power *from* disputed land features at the peril of smaller claimant states and, arguably, freedom of (military) navigation and overflight in the area.[9]

More troublingly, China has rapidly "weaponized" its artificial islands through the deployment of advanced assets, including HQ-9B surface-to-air-missiles, YJ-12B anti-cruise ballistic missiles, and electronic jamming equipment to the Spratlys, while conducting increasingly regular large-

scale military exercises across the South China Sea.[10] And more recently, we
have witnessed what can be termed China's "militia-zation"[11] of disputes—
deploying an ever-larger number of para-military forces to swarm and
intimidate smaller claimant states at sea. In the first few months of 2019
alone, Beijing deployed an armada of up to 275 individual Chinese vessels
over a span of three months, which laid siege on the Philippine-occupied
Thitu Island in the Spratlys.[12]

This represents a new and dangerous phase in China's maritime policy
in the South China Sea, as rivals scramble to construct an appropriate
response without provoking unnecessary escalation. The militia forces,
however, continue to represent the tip of the dagger of China's modernizing conventional forces. In short, we are seeing a new China, which is no
longer bound by Deng Xiaoping's dictum of strategic temperance, namely
to "hide our capabilities and bide our time, [and] never try to take the
lead." Instead, China is driven by a new level of assertiveness embodied by
Xi Jinping's bid for a "Chinese Dream" of "great [national] rejuvenation"—
namely, Chinese strategic primacy in the 21st century.[13]

CONSTRAINTMENT, NOT CONTAINMENT

None of China's remarkable achievements, however, necessarily portend
Chinese world domination, not even hegemony in Asia.[14] To begin with,
China suffers from acute structural vulnerabilities, including an impend-
ing demographic winter[15] (that is, that the aging population will surpass
the working population within this decade) and excessively leveraged financial sector, which foretell an almost inevitable economic slowdown,[16]
if not worse, in the short to medium term.[17] An examination of actual
Chinese power—its net power of surplus resources,[18] as opposed to gross
resources for force projection during war—reveal a significant, if not widening, gap with more developed rivals such as the United States, which
still boasts the largest pool of cutting-edge industries, Nobel laureates,
high-quality human capital, and strategic natural resources.[19]

As structural realities catch up with China's maturing economy, and
the specter of a "middle-income trap" haunts the once-booming nation,
calls for foreign policy moderation, reduced defense spending, and recon-
figuration of the BRI and other ambitious overseas projects are bound to
intensify. Xi would reserve the potentially disastrous rally 'round the flag

option were the domestic situation to sink to a state of political despera-
tion, calling for unity by engaging in jingoistic and ethnocentric nationalistic discourse, as we have seen during Hong Kong protests and more
recently amid the pandemic.[20] More crucially, China's geopolitical assertiveness has provoked backlash across the Indo-Pacific, most prominently
in the United States, where there is an emerging bipartisan consensus on
the need to craft a robust corresponding strategy. In a sign of the changing times, even former Treasury secretary and Goldman Sachs executive
Henry Paulson, a former economic advisor to China and a long-time advocate for "constructive cooperation" with Beijing,[21] has warned of an "economic iron curtain."[22] Similar anxieties have influenced threat perceptions
vis-à-vis China among other major players,[23] including Japan, India, and
the European Union, which have stepped up their military presence and
strategic countermeasures in the Asia-Pacific region.[24]

At the same time, the fundamental geopolitical reality is that China
is simply too big to be "contained" in the George Kennan–like Cold War
fashion of the twentieth century.[25] And unlike the Soviet Union, China
is deeply embedded in and pivotal to the global economy.[26] Instead, a
more feasible alternative is what political scientist Gerald Segal termed as
"constrainment" strategy, which "is intended to tell [China] that the outside world has interests that will be defended by means of incentives for
good behavior, deterrence of bad behavior, and punishment when deterrence fails."[27] This approach, as Segal argues, will work if the United States
and its partners "act in a concerted fashion both to punish and to reward
China."[28] In many ways, the U.S. push for a rules-based Free and Open
Indo-Pacific (FOIP) resembles a constrainment strategy against China.[29]
It draws on a combination of diplomatic pressure, economic cooperation,
and deepening military countermeasures in tandem with likeminded
powers, which have been perturbed by a revisonist China's frontal challenge to the existing order.

THE SPECTER OF THE COLD WAR

In Southeast Asia, however, the whole Indo-Pacific and FOIP discourse[30]
is often seen, rather skeptically, as thinly veiled containment strategy[31] by
the so-called Quad grouping of Australia, Japan, India, and the United
States against a revanchist China.[32] There is profound anxiety over broader

implications for ASEAN and its "centrality" in shaping the regional security architecture. From a more skeptical standpoint, many in Southeast Asians even interpret the Indo-Pacific—and the corollary reemergence of the Quad[33]—as de facto marginalization of ASEAN, with big powers effectively stating: "Step aside little guys, let the big boys handle this China problem!" A fog of uncertainty is fueling suspicion and dismay. To begin with, there is general perplexity vis-à-vis the whole Indo-Pacific concept and, by extension, what the FOIP truly stands for. After all, as Southeast Asia expert Hoang Thi Ha notes: "There is no common understanding or authoritative definition of the term even among its proponents."[34]

Beyond a conceptual vacuum, however, ASEAN is already profoundly worried by the prospect of an institutional vacuum, which would pave the way for naked great power rivalry. ASEAN's fears of a return to Cold War, zero-sum geopolitics is far from baseless. The Trump administration's National Security Strategy (NSS) suggests Washington's full embrace of a great-powers-centered paradigm, where Beijing is a "revisionist" power that seeks to "challenge American power, influence, and interests" across the Indo-Pacific and beyond "to erode American security and prosperity."[35] In its National Defense Strategy (NDS), the Pentagon, in turn, accuses Beijing of "leveraging military modernization, influence operations, and predatory economics to coerce continues its neighboring countries to reorder the Indo-Pacific region to their advantage" and "continu[ing] to pursue a military modernization program that seeks Indo-Pacific regional hegemony in the future" through the "displacement of the United States to achieve global preeminence in the future."[36]

Such official lexicon, highlighting the struggle for primacy between the United States and China, eerily echoes Cold War rhetoric and, by extension, revives dark memories of a brutal past in Southeast Asian collective consciousness. This is precisely why ASEAN constantly emphasizes its unwllingness to choose between competing sides.[37] After all, its very post–Cold War raison d'être has been the prevention of a return to the old days of bipolar superpower competition.[38]

In response to (real and perceived) threats to an ASEAN-anchored regional security architecture, Indonesia—the reticent natural leader in Southeast Asia and cradle of the "third way" Non-Aligned Movement (NAM)—has pushed for ASEAN's own definition of the Indo-Pacific. The aim is for ASEAN to play a pivotal role in shaping the contours of the emerging regional security architecture and its underlying values. In recent years, the Indonesian Foreign Minister Retno Marsudi has advocated for an alternative conception, which is "open, transparent and inclusive" and espouses "the habit of dialogue, promoting cooperation and friendship, and upholding international law."[39] This builds on the efforts of her dynamic predecessor, Marty Natalegawa, who devoted significant diplomatic capital to promoting ASEAN centrality in the past decade.[40] Indonesia's efforts reached an apotheosis in the ASEAN Summit in Bangkok in June 2019, when Southeast Asian nations adopted the ASEAN Outlook on the Indo-Pacific (AOIP). [41]

From Jakarta's (and ASEAN's by extension) standpoint, China is not a monolithic "revisionist" power, but instead a core element of the emerging regional security architecture. For Southeast Asian countries, Beijing is an indispensable stakeholder, which has to be engaged on an institutionalized, if not conciliatory, basis—and perhaps even primarily through ASEAN mechanisms.[42] ASEAN categorically rejects any narrow definition of China as a hegemonic threat that has to be contained by a counter-coalition of powers. In short, ASEAN primarily views China through the prism of money (engagement-economic axis) rather than missiles (threat-deterrence axis).

The AOIP calls for an ASEAN that will "continue to maintain its central role in the evolving regional architecture in Southeast Asia and its surrounding regions" and serve as an "an honest broker within the strategic environment of competing interests." The AOIP underscores ASEAN's commitment to an "open," "transparent," "inclusive," "rules-based" order anchored by "respect for international law."[43] It reaffirms ASEAN's long-held post–Cold War aspiration to "lead the shaping of their economic and security architecture and ensure that such dynamics will continue to bring about peace, security, stability and prosperity for the peoples in the Southeast Asia as well as in the wider Asia-Pacific and Indian Ocean regions or the Indo-Pacific." And it underscores ASEAN's pacifist values and emphasis on conflict-prevention and management through "avoiding the deepening of mistrust, miscalculation, and patterns of behavior based on a zero-sum game."

But the AOIP appears at best defensive and, at worst, a desperate attempt at reasserting ASEAN centrality. Instead of just *asserting* centrality, and engaging in hermeneutic debates on its laudable geopolitical aspirations, ASEAN should *achieve and earn* a pivotal role in shaping the emerging twenty-first-century order in the Indo-Pacific. The reality is that ASEAN's refusal to choose on pivotal geopolitical issues represents a choice itself, potentially leading to its peripherality in regional affairs. And in many ways, ASEAN facilitates China's revanchism by its stubborn neutrality. Not to mention that ASEAN has chosen sides on certain issues already, having criticized the United States and India, the other two major regional powers, on trade protectionism issues.[44]

THE INEVITABLE CHOICE

The path forward should begin by first acknowledging and, accordingly, remedying ASEAN's institutional decay. To be fair, ASEAN has had remarkable achievements, especially ending the dark days of *Konfrontasi*[45] and intra-regional armed conflict as well as finalizing the ASEAN Free Trade Area ahead of schedule.[46] It also boasts a myriad of assets, especially its convening power:[47] namely, the establishment and preservation of multilateral mechanisms, which have mediated, with considerable success, broadly peaceful relations among great powers. The ASEAN Regional Forum (ARF) is among few multilateral platforms where all major Indo-Pacific powers and actors, including North Korea, can collectively negotiate the rules governing interstate relations in the Indo-Pacific.

Yet, ASEAN is credibly suffering from what can be termed as a "middle institutionalization trap."[48] The very decisionmaking modalities and institutional arrangements that allowed ASEAN to integrate among the world's most diverse nations are proving insufficient, if not counterproductive, vis-à-vis new geopolitical realities, namely the rise of China. In particular, ASEAN's operational interpretation of consensus (*Muafakat*) as unanimity, especially in the realm of politico-security affairs, has proven to be a recipe for division, dissonance, and collective paralysis. In contrast, other reigonal organizations such as the European Union have operationalized the consensus principle through more optimal arrangements, including qualified majority voting.[49] ASEAN's unanimity-based decisionmaking process gives de facto veto power to each ASEAN member irrespective of the immense divergence in threat perceptions and degree of interest among Southeast Asian nations. This makes the regional body extremely vulnerable to sabotage,[50] since an external power can simply lean on the "weak links" within the regional body to prevent a unified pushback.

If anything, this arrangement is even unfair to countries such as Cambodia, a member state heavily susceptible to Chinese pressure due to its reliance on Beijing's economic assistance.[51] This is precisely why Cambodian Prime Minister Hun Sen has repeatedly sought to either shun or block a robust ASEAN position on maritime disputes, where it has no direct national interest.[52] As he complained amid ASEAN debates over the South China Sea arbitration case at The Hague against China: "It is very unjust for Cambodia, using Cambodia to counter China. They use us and curse us . . . this is not about laws, it is totally about politics."[53]

Key American allies, meanwhile, have proven equally unreliable. This is clearly the case in President Rodrigo Duterte's dramatic reversal of longstanding Philippine strategic orientation by embracing a full-fledged China-leaning policy. Though bilateral defense ties with the United States have remained robust, Duterte has echoed Chinese talking points by insisting that the South China Sea disputes are "better left untouched"[54] by external powers. Even to chagrin of his own people,[55] he has gone so far as to effectively "set aside"[56] the 2016 landmark arbitration award,[57] which unambiguously nullified China's expansive claims and aggressive behavior in adjacent waters.

Even more troublingly, the Duterte administration has welcomed joint development agreements with Beijing in contested waters. But this potentially violates both the Philippines' own constitution as well as the 2016 arbitral ruling, legitimizing China's expansive claims in the area.[58] It also emboldens China's controversial demand[59] for exclusive sharing of resources within the South China Sea basin under an emerging Code of Conduct (COC) with ASEAN—a process currently overseen by the Philippines as the ASEAN-China country coordinator. The upshot of Duterte's actions is the further weakening of ASEAN's hand on arguably the most crucial flashpoint—the "Thucydides trap"—of our times.[60] But not all is lost. In contrast to the Philippines and Cambodia, historically nonaligned Muslim nations of Malaysia and Indonesia have begun to step up their resistance to Chinese maritime intrusions like never before.

In December, Malaysia directly challenged China's claims in the southern portions of the South China Sea but submitting its extended continental shelf at the United Nations.[61] When Beijing furiously criticized the move,[62] Malaysian Foreign Minister Saifuddin Abdullah immediately shot back by dismissing China's expansive claims as "ridiculous."[63] He even warned of international "arbitration" to assert Malaysia's maritime rights and claims against China, if necessary.[64] Shortly after, Indonesia joined the fray by openly questioning China's claims off the coast of the Natuna Islands, which overlap with the southern tip of the nine-dash line. In uncharacteristically strident language, the Indonesian Foreign Ministry accused China of "violation of [its] sovereignty" and, invoking the 2016 arbitral tribunal ruling, questioned the latter's claims in the area as having "no legal basis" in the United Nations Convention on the Law of the Sea (UNCLOS).[65]

In response to the intrusion of dozens of Chinese para-military and fishing vessels into Indonesia's territorial sea, Jakarta has bolstered its military presence around the Natuna Islands, while President Joko Widodo made a high-profile visit to the islands, where he warned China: "We have a district here, a regent, and a governor here. There are no more debates. De facto, de jure, Natuna is Indonesia."[66] Shortly before assuming the chairmanship of ASEAN this year, Vietnam threatened "arbitration and litigation measures" to constrain China's aggressive behavior in adjacent waters.[67] Emboldened by the Philippines' successful precedence,[68] Vietnamese academics[69] have publicly supported compulsory arbitration as a potential countermeasure, especially in light of the months-long naval showdown over the Vanguard Bank last year.[70]

The challenge for Vietnam, the current ASEAN chair, is to harmonize divergent positions within the region vis-à-vis the South China Sea disputes. While Malaysia and Indonesia have stepped up their efforts to resist Chinese intrusion into their waters, the Philippines' strategic acquiescence remains to be a major obstacle to a unified and robust regional pushback against Beijing's worst instincts. Fortunately, recent history shows that China responds to robust pressure, while the Philippines' position is far from fixed. From its decision to forego veto powers[71] within the Asian Infrastructure Investment Bank amid Western pushback to greater emphasis on debt sustainability and major concessions to Malaysia over "debt trap" concerns vis-à-vis the Belt and Road Initiative,[72] Beijing has shown its willingness to recalibrate in face of concerted pushback. One reason China has refused to specify the precise coordinates of its nine-dash line claims is because it wants to maintain space for negotiations down the road.[73] Absent a coordinated and coherent resistance among key regional states, China will likely continue its current course of transforming the regional maritime and geopolitical landscape in its own image.

RECOMMENDATIONS

■ **Optimizing consensus-building:** The way forward is for ASEAN to contemplate alternative and more optimal decisionmaking modalities, including the expanded adoption of the "ASEAN Minus X" formula,[74] namely majority-based voting, which proved successful in trade negotiations. More ambitiously, ASEAN can examine the utility of the qualified majority voting modality,[75] which incorporates differential (demographic, economic, geopolitical) weight of member states.

■ **Embracing minilateralism:** Crucially, ASEAN can more proactively adopt "minilateralism," whereby core, like-minded Southeast Asian countries can adopt more expedient and robust responses to shared threats, including in cooperation with external powers. In recent years, we have seen "osmotic integration," most notably in the case of the ASEAN Counter-Terrorism Convention,[76] where minilateral arrangements were later adopted on the collective, multilateral level. Minilateral initiatives such as Indonesian President Joko Widodo's call for joint patrols,[77] Malaysian Prime Minister Mahathir Mohamad's call for demilitarization in disputed waters, and the proposal for an intra-ASEAN COC,[78] anchored by the UNCLOS, seem much more sensible and promising than the status quo.

■ **Expanded partnerships:** Perhaps, the time has also come for considering the impossible, namely negotiating associate membership[79] for "far neighbors" such as Australia and New Zealand. ASEAN will either have to embrace creative solutions or risk fast fading into irrelevance amid festering Sino-American competition in the Indo-Pacific.[80] Crucially, it is important for the Quad powers to continue and deepen their capacity-building initiatives in Southeast Asia, particulalry maritime security capabilities of frontline states such as the Philippines, Vietnam, Malaysia, and Indonesia, which have been grappling and even resisting Chinese maritime aggression.

Notes

1. Henry Kissinger, *World Order* (London: Penguin Books, 2014), 365.

2. The "Beijing Consensus," a term coined by Joshua Cooper-Ramo and further developed by Sinologists such as Stefan Halper, pertains to China's no-strings-attached, flexible approach to international trade and investment relations. Unlike the West and international financial institutions such as the International Monetary and World Bank, which have aggressively espoused structural adjustment programs and pro-market governance reforms in accordance with the neo-liberal principles of what John Williamson calls the "Washington Consensus," China does not demand drastic economic (or political) reforms when it engages in trade and investment with other countries. And this, for some experts, explains China's special attractiveness as an economic partner to many countries. Joshua Ramo, "Beijing Consensus," The Foreign Policy Centre, November 5, 2004, http://www.xuanju.org/uploadfile/200909/20090918021638239.pdf.

3. Graham Allison and Robert Blackwill, "Interview: Lee Kuan Yew on the Future of U.S.-China Relations," *The Atlantic*, March 5, 2013, https://www.theatlantic.com/china/archive/2013/03/interview-lee-kuan-yew-on-the-future-of-us-china-relations/273657/.

4. Daniel H. Nexon, "The Balance of Power in the Balance," *World Politics* 61, no. 2 (2009): 330–59, http://www.jstor.org/stable/40263485.

5. T. J. Ma, "Empty trains on the modern Silk Road: when Belt and Road interests don't align," Panda Paw Dragon Claw, August 23, 2019, https://pandapawdragonclaw.blog/2019/08/23/empty-trains-on-the-modern-silk-road-when-belt-and-road-interests-dont-align/.

6. Peter Cai, ""Understanding China's Belt and Road Initiative," The Lowy Institute, March 22, 2017, https://www.lowyinstitute.org/publications/understanding-belt-and-road-initiative.

7. Bruno Maçães, *Belt and Road: A Chinese World Order* (London: Hurst, 2019).

8. "China's 'maritime road' looks more defensive than imperialist," *The Economist*, September 28, 2019, https://www.economist.com/graphic-detail/2019/09/28/chinas-maritime-road-looks-more-defensive-than-imperialist.

9. Gregory Poling, "Conventional Wisdom on China's Island Bases is Dangerously Wrong," War on the Rocks, January 10, 2020, https://warontherocks.com/2020/01/the-conventional-wisdom-on-chinas-island-bases-is-dangerously-wrong/.

10. Richard Javad Heydarian, "Duterte and the Philippines' contested foreign policy," Asia Maritime Transparency Initiative, August 20, 2018, https://amti.csis.org/duterte-philippines-contested-foreign-policy/.

11. Richard Heydarian, "Why China's 'militiasation' of the South China Sea needs a review by the Philippines-US alliance," *South China Morning Post*, July 20, 2019, https://www.scmp.com/news/china/diplomacy/article/3019060/why-chinas-militiasation-south-china-sea-needs-review.

12. Julie Aurelio, "PH protests presence of Chinese boats near Pag-asa," Inquirer, April 2, 2019, https://globalnation.inquirer.net/174045/ph-protests-presence-of-chinese-boats-near-pag-asa.

13. Elizabeth Economy, *The Third Revolution: Xi Jingping and the New Chinese State* (Oxford: Oxford University Press, 2018).

14. Martin Jacques, *When China Rules the World: The End of the Western World and the Birth of a New Global Order: Second Edition* (London: Penguin Books, 2012).

15. Steven Lee Myers, Jin Wu, and Claire Fu, "China's Looming Crisis: A Shrinking Population," *The New York Times*, January 17, 2020, https://www.nytimes.com/interactive/2019/01/17/world/asia/china-population-crisis.html.

16. Ruchie Sharma, *Breakout Nations: In Pursuit of the Next Economic Miracles* (New York: W.W. Norton & Company, 2012).

17. Salvatore Babones, "China Hits the Wall," *Foreign Affairs*, August 16, 2015, https://www.foreignaffairs.com/articles/china/2015-08-16/china-hits-wall.

18. Michael Beckley, "China's Century: Why America's Edge Will Endure," *International Security* 36 no. 3 (2011/2012), 41–78, https://www.mitpressjournals.org/doi/pdf/10.1162/ISEC_a_00066.

19. Michael Beckley, *Unrivaled: Why America Will Remain the World's Sole Superpower* (New York: Cornell University Press, 2018).

20. Suzanne Nossel, "China Is Fighting the Coronavirus Propaganda War to Win," *Foreign Policy*, March 20, 2020, https://foreignpolicy.com/2020/03/20/china-coronavirus-propaganda-war-journalists-press-freedom/.

21. Henry Paulson, *Dealing with China: An Insider Unmasks the New Economic Superpower* (New York: Twelve, 2016).

22. Jamil Anderlini, "American executives are becoming China sceptics," *Financial Times*, November 14, 2018, https://www.ft.com/content/389a92c2-e738-11e8-8a85-04b8afea6ea3.

23. Richard Javad Heydarian, "China's new abnormal: European patrols in disputed Southeast Asian waters," *South China Morning Post*, June 15, 2019, https://www.scmp.com/news/china/diplomacy/article/3014264/chinas-new-abnormal-european-patrols-disputed-southeast-asian.

24. Lee Jeong-ho and Keegan Elmer, "European nations 'determined to stay relevant' in Asia-Pacific, South China Sea," *South China Morning Post*, September 15, 2019, https://www.scmp.com/news/china/diplomacy/article/3027256/european-nations-determined-stay-relevant-asia-pacific-south.

25. George Kennan, "CONTAINMENT: 40 Years Later: The Sources of Soviet Conduct," *Foreign Affairs* (1987), https://www.foreignaffairs.com/articles/russia-fsu/1987-03-01/containment-40-years-later-sources-soviet-conduct.

26. Stephen Roach, "Why China is central to global growth," World Economic Forum, September 2, 2016, https://www.weforum.org/agenda/2016/09/why-china-is-central-to-global-growth;%20https://www.theatlantic.com/international/archive/2015/09/united-states-china-war-thucydides-trap/406756/.

27. Gerald Segal, "East Asia and the 'Constrainment' of China," *International Security* 20, no. 4 (1996): 107-35, https://www.jstor.org/stable/2539044?seq=1.

28. Gerald Segal, "East Asia and the "Constrainment" of China."

29. Jeff M. Smith, "Unpacking the Free and Open Indo-Pacific," War on the Rocks, March 14, 2018, https://warontherocks.com/2018/03/unpacking-the-free-and-open-indo-pacific/.

30. Hoang Thi Ha, "ASEAN Outlook on the Indo-Pacific: Old Wine in New Bottle?," ISEAS Yusof Ishak Institute, June 25, 2019, https://www.iseas.edu.sg/images/pdf/ISEAS_Perspective_2019_51.pdf.

31. George Kennan, "The Sources of Soviet Conduct," *Foreign Affairs* (1947), https://www.foreignaffairs.com/articles/russian-federation/1947-07-01/sources-soviet-conduct.

32. Tanvi Madan, "'The Rise, Fall and Rebirth of the 'Quad,'" War on the Rocks, November 16, 2017, https://warontherocks.com/2017/11/rise-fall-rebirth-quad/.

33. Tanvi Madan, "The Rise, Fall and Rebirth of the 'Quad.'"

34. Hoang Thi Ha, "ASEAN Outlook on the Indo-Pacific: Old Wine in New Bottle?"

35. "National Security Strategy of the United States of America," 2017, https://www.whitehouse.gov/wp-content/uploads/2017/12/NSS-Final-12-18-2017-0905.pdf.

36. "Indo-Pacific Strategy Report," U.S. Department of Defense, 2019, https://media.defense.gov/2019/Jul/01/2002152311/-1/-1/1/DEPARTMENT-OF-DEFENSE-INDO-PACIFIC-STRATEGY-REPORT-2019.PDF.

37. Jonathan Stromseth, "Don't make us choose: Southeast Asia in the throes of US-China rivalry" (Washington, DC: The Brookings Institution, October 2019), https://www.brookings.edu/research/dont-make-us-choose-southeast-asia-in-the-throes-of-us-china-rivalry/.

38. Amitav Acharya, "A new regional order in South-East Asia: ASEAN in the post-cold war era: Introduction," *The Adelphi Papers* 33 no. 279 (2008): 3–6, https://doi.org/10.1080/05679329308449177.

39. Agnes Anya, "East Asia to hear about Indo-Pacific idea," *The Jakarta Post*, May 9, 2018, https://www.thejakartapost.com/news/2018/05/09/east-asia-hear-about-indo-pacific-idea.html.

40. Nyshka Chandran, "As Pence kicks off his Asia tour, other countries have their own ideas for the 'Indo-Pacific,'" CNBC News, November 11, 2018, https://www.cnbc.com/2018/11/12/us-japan-and-indonesia-set-their-sights-on-the-indo-pacific-region.html.

41. "ASEAN Outlook on the Indo-Pacific," ASEAN, June 2019, https://asean.org/storage/2019/06/ASEAN-Outlook-on-the-Indo-Pacific_FINAL_22062019.pdf.

42. Richard Javad Heydarian, "ASEAN Chooses to Focus on Chinese Money over Missiles," China-US Focus, May 9, 2018, https://www.chinausfocus.com/foreign-policy/asean-chooses-to-focus-on-chinese-money-over-missiles.

43. Hoang Thi Ha, "ASEAN Outlook on the Indo-Pacific: Old Wine in New Bottle?"

44. Kim Jaewon, "South Korea and ASEAN vow to resist Trump-style protectionism," *Nikkei Asia*, November 26, 2019, https://asia.nikkei.com/Economy/Trade-war/South-Korea-and-ASEAN-vow-to-resist-Trump-style-protectionism.

45. Adam Leong Kok Wey, "The War That Gave Birth to ASEAN," *The Diplomat*, September 6, 2016, https://thediplomat.com/2016/09/the-war-that-gave-birth-to-asean/.

46. See Hadi Soesastro, "The ASEAN Free Trade: A Critical Assessment," *The*

Journal of East Asian Affairs 16 no. 1 (2002): 20–53, https://www.jstor.org/stable/23255936?seq=1; "Riding the ASEAN elephant," *The Economist*, 2013, http://ftp01.economist.com.hk/ECN_papers/ridingASEAN.pdf; Richard Javad Heydarian, "The ASEAN plus three holds the key to globalization's future," CGTN, August 1, 2019, https://news.cgtn.com/news/2019-08-01/The-ASEAN-plus-three-holds-the-key-to-globalization-s-future-INmQdFNvm8/index.html.

47. Lindsey Ford, "Does ASEAN Matter?," Asia Society Policy Institute, November 12, 2018, https://asiasociety.org/policy-institute/does-asean-matter.

48. Richard Javad Heydarian, "Duterte and the Philippines' contested foreign policy," Asia Maritime Transparency Initiative, August 20, 2018, https://amti.csis.org/duterte-philippines-contested-foreign-policy/.

49. For more details on qualified majority voting, see "New Council qualified majority Voting Rules In effect," Council of the European Union, December 4, 2014, https://www.consilium.europa.eu/en/documents-publications/library/library-blog/posts/new-council-qualified-majority-voting-rules-in-effect/.

50. Somethea Tann, "How Chinese money is changing Cambodia," *Deutsche Welle*, August 22, 2019, https://www.dw.com/en/how-chinese-money-is-changing-cambodia/a-50130240.

51. Nem Sopheakpanha, "China Pledges $10 Billion in Support to Cambodia as Relations With West Deteriorate," Voice of America, January 23, 2019, https://www.voacambodia.com/a/china-pledges-10-billion-in-support-to-cambodia-as-relations-with-west-deteriorate/4755548.html.

52. AFP, Ananth Baliga, and Vong Sokheng, "Cambodia again blocks ASEAN statement on South China Sea," *The Phnom Penh Post*, July 25, 2016, https://www.phnompenhpost.com/national/cambodia-again-blocks-asean-statement-south-china-sea.

53. Agence France-Presse, "Furious Cambodian premier Hun Sen highlights ASEAN splits over South China Sea disputes," *South China Morning Post*, June 20, 2016, https://www.scmp.com/news/asia/east-asia/article/1978092/furious-cambodian-premier-hun-sen-highlights-asean-splits-over.

54. Shi Jiangtao and Liu Zhen, "'Better left untouched': Philippines and Vietnam wary of Trump offer to mediate South China Sea disputes," *South China Morning Post*, November 12, 2017, https://www.scmp.com/news/china/diplomacy-defence/article/2119551/better-left-untouched-philippines-and-vietnam-wary.

55. See Sofia Tomacruz, "3 years later, 87% of Filipinos want gov't to assert Hague ruling," Rappler, July 12, 2019, https://www.rappler.com/nation/235259-filipinos-want-government-assert-hague-ruling-sws-survey-2019.

56. Virgil Lopez, "Duterte considers setting aside arbitral ruling for economic gain," GMA News, September 11, 2019, https://www.gmanetwork.com/news/news/nation/707643/duterte-considers-setting-aside-arbitral-ruling-for-economic-gain/story/.

57. Richard Javad Heydarian, "The day after: Enforcing The Hague verdict in the South China Sea" (Washington, DC: The Brookings Institution, July 25, 2016), https://www.brookings.edu/opinions/the-day-after-enforcing-the-hague-verdict-in-the-south-china-sea/.

58. Richard Javad Heydarian, "Crossing the Rubicon: Duterte, China and Resource-Sharing in the South China Sea," Maritime Issues, October 23, 2018, http://www.maritimeissues.com/politics/crossing-the-rubicon-duterte-china-and-resourcesharing-in-the-south-china-sea.html.

59. Carl Thayer, "A Closer Look at the ASEAN-China Single Draft South China Sea Code of Conduct," *The Diplomat*, August 3, 2018, https://thediplomat.com/2018/08/a-closer-look-at-the-asean-china-single-draft-south-china-sea-code-of-conduct/.

60. Graham Allison, "The Thucydides Trap," *Foreign Policy*, June 9, 2017, https://foreignpolicy.com/2017/06/09/the-thucydides-trap/.

61. "Malaysia Partial Submission to the Commission on the Limits of the Continental Shelf pursuant to Article 76, paragraph 8 of the United Nations Convention on the Law of the Sea 1982 in the South China Sea," United Nations, November 2017, https://www.un.org/Depts/los/clcs_new/submissions_files/mys85_2019/20171128_MYS_ES_DOC_001_secured.pdf.

62. Laura Zhou, "Beijing urges UN commission not to consider Malaysian claim in South China Sea," *South China Morning Post*, December 17, 2019, https://www.scmp.com/news/china/diplomacy/article/3042333/beijing-urges-un-commission-not-consider-malaysian-claim-south.

63. Ted Regencia, "Malaysia FM: China's 'nine-dash line' claim 'ridiculous,'" Aljazeera, December 21, 2019, https://www.aljazeera.com/news/2019/12/malaysian-top-envoy-china-dash-line-claim-ridiculous-191221034730108.html.

64. "Malaysia does not fear China reprisals over disputed area claim, says foreign minister," Malaymail, January 3, 2020, https://www.malaymail.com/amp/news/malaysia/2020/01/03/malaysia-does-not-fear-china-retaliation-over-disputed-area-claim-says-fore/1824429?fbclid=IwAR1Zt2PSJzU43kjm52fEbaTKn2YABKBKpC8 5iOtBrdl2Wf1Td4rdTIsdmNc.

65. Kinling Lo, "How Indonesia's South China Sea dispute with Beijing could lead to tough Asean stance on code of conduct," *South China Morning Post*, January 2, 2020, https://www.scmp.com/news/china/diplomacy/article/3044374/how-indonesias-south-china-sea-dispute-beijing-could-lead.

66. Fransiska Nangoy, Wilda Asmarini, Stanley Widianto, and Gabriel Crossley, "Indonesia's president visits island in waters disputed by China," Reuters, January 8, 2020, https://www.reuters.com/article/us-indonesia-china-southchinasea/indonesias-president-visits-island-in-waters-disputed-by-china-idUSKBN1Z710N.

67. James Pearson and Khanh Vu, "Vietnam mulls legal action over South China Sea dispute," Reuters, November 6, 2019, https://www.reuters.com/article/us-vietnam-southchinasea/vietnam-mulls-legal-action-over-south-china-sea-dispute-idUSKBN1XG1D6.

68. Richard Javad Heydarian, "Vietnam's Legal Warfare against China: Prospects and Challenges," Asia Maritime Transparency Initiative, November 21, 2019, https://amti.csis.org/vietnams-legal-warfare-against-china-prospects-and-challenges/.

69. Joshua Lipes, "Experts Call For Vietnam to Sue China in International Court Over South China Sea Incursions," Radio Free Asia, October 9, 2019, https://www.rfa.org/english/news/vietnam/lawsuit-10092019152725.html/.

70. Sreenivasa Rao Pemmaraju, "The South China Sea Arbitration (The

Philippines v. China): Assessment of the Award on Jurisdiction and Admissibility," Chinese Journal of International Law 15 no. 2 (2016): 265–307, https://doi.org/10.1093/chinesejil/jmw019.

71. Lingline Wei and Bob Davis, "China Forgoes Veto Power at New Bank to Win Key European Nations' Support," *Wall Street Journal*, March 23, 2015, https://www.wsj.com/articles/china-forgoes-veto-power-at-new-bank-to-win-key-european-nations-support-1427131055.

72. Alexandra Stevenson, "China Yields on Malaysia Rail Project as Global Infrastructure Program Is Re-Examined," *The New York Times*, April 12, 2019, https://www.nytimes.com/2019/04/12/business/chinese-high-speed-rail-malaysia.html.

73. Based on the author's conversations with senior Chinese experts and officials between 2014 and 2019, including twice in the Chinese Foreign Ministry in Beijing.

74. Ralf Emmers, "ASEAN minus X: Should This Formula Be Extended?," S. Rajaratnam School of International Studies (RSIS) , October 24, 2017, https://www.rsis.edu.sg/rsis-publication/cms/co17199-asean-minus-x-should-this-formula-be-extended/#.XZ_2EFUzbIU.

75. "Voting system: Qualified Majority," European Council, https://www.consilium.europa.eu/en/council-eu/voting-system/qualified-majority/.

76. Ralf Emmers, "ASEAN minus X: Should This Formula Be Extended?"

77. "Jokowi to discuss S. China Sea joint patrols with Turnbull," Today Online, February 25, 2017, https://www.todayonline.com/world/asia/jokowi-discuss-s-china-sea-joint-patrols-turnbull.

78. Tashny Sukumaran, "Mahathir to update Malaysia's foreign policy, including on South China Sea and international Muslim cooperation," *South China Sea Morning Post*, September 19, 2019, https://www.scmp.com/week-asia/politics/article/3027949/mahathir-update-malaysias-foreign-policy-including-south-china.

79. Graeme Dobell, "Australia as an ASEAN Community partner," Australian Strategic Policy Institute, February 20, 2018, https://www.aspi.org.au/report/australia-asean-community-partner.

80. Richard Javad Heydarian, "Australia right to huddle closer to Southeast Asia," *Nikkei Asia*, March 20, 2018, https://asia.nikkei.com/Politics/International-relations/Australia-right-to-huddle-closer-to-Southeast-Asia.

4

The Case for an Australian Step-Up in Southeast Asia

HERVÉ LEMAHIEU

THE THREE THEATERS OF AUSTRALIA'S INDO-PACIFIC STRATEGY

Australia has long been spoiled by its splendid isolation—surrounded as it is by friends and fish across two oceans, the Indian and the Pacific. This offers a comparative advantage relative to many Asian counterparts, whose geographies play far more directly into their strategic vulnerability.

Nevertheless, managing relations in the multiple neighborhoods surrounding the island continent also poses unique challenges for a middle power with limited resources. Australia's prosperity is inextricably invested in the security of both the Indian and Pacific oceans as well as maritime and continental Southeast Asia. This helps explain why Canberra was an early adopter of the Indo-Pacific concept as an organizing principle for its foreign and defense policy.

The Australian Department of Foreign Affairs and Trade's 2017 Foreign Policy White Paper lays out the following overarching aim in the extended region: "To support a balance in the Indo-Pacific favourable to our interests and promote an open, inclusive and rules-based region."[1] This chapter broadly identifies three geographic "rings" of Australian strategic interests, each defined by a distinct set of foreign policy and defense objectives, that together frame Australia's Indo-Pacific strategy:

■ **A Pacific "inner ring" where Australia is the dominant resident power and will, alone if necessary, use military force to safeguard its interests and regional stability.** Australia's near abroad encompasses its northern approaches through to the small island states of the South Pacific. For much of the twentieth century, including World War II, Papua New Guinea was Australia's "northern shield."[2] Today Papua New Guinea continues to reinforce the imagined boundary of Australia's "inner ring."[3]

■ **A Southeast Asian "middle ring" where Australia must work "with and through equals" to pursue an inclusive and rules-based regional order.**[4] Southeast Asia "frames Australia's northern approaches" and most important trade routes, and "sits at a nexus of strategic competition in the Indo-Pacific," according to the 2017 Foreign Policy White Paper.[5] Australia and the emerging middle powers of Southeast Asia alike are struggling to deal with the erosion of the rules-based order in the face of the realignment of U.S.-China relations.

■ **An Indo-Pacific "outer ring" where Australia is working with Japan, India, and the United States to create a military and strategic counterweight to China.** Australia's quadrilateral grouping with three major Indo-Pacific powers, including its longstanding ally the United States, is the standard-bearer for its emerging regional defense diplomacy. The aim here is to deepen military cooperation among like-minded democracies to signal an intent to counter and thereby deter future Chinese attempts to further alter the status quo in the Indo-Pacific.

MIDDLE-POWER DIPLOMACY

In calling for an "open, inclusive and rules-based" Indo-Pacific, Australia has sought to emphasize only the most vital overlapping interests of open trade, inclusive regionalism, and basic respect for territorial and domestic sovereignty among a broad church of actors across these concentric theaters.

Such pragmatism is designed in part to encourage middle-power cooperation and its role in region-building. Rory Medcalf, a leading Australian advocate for the Indo-Pacific concept, has used the idea to seek to move the Australian debate from a narrow "U.S. versus China" lens to one that properly puts the entire region into discussions of regional order.[6] He argues that Australian foreign policy should be premised on the potential of middle powers to achieve significant things, both in the absence of the United States as a regional security guarantor and in open defiance of China as an economic powerhouse.

The findings of the Lowy Institute's Asia Power Index appear to support this view.[7] When neither the United States nor China can "win" primacy in Asia, the actions of the next rung of powers become more consequential and will constitute the marginal difference. A balance of power will ultimately be determined not simply by rival superpowers but the interests and choices of a "long tail" of large and small powers. These actors can collectively influence the regional order, even if none is powerful enough to attempt to dictate it.

A SOUTHEAST ASIA STEP BACK?

Both the 2016 Defence White Paper and the 2017 Foreign Policy White Paper suggest that Australia's government should weigh its geographical theaters and priorities equally in support of "a stable Indo-Pacific region and a rules-based global order."[8] However, this chapter argues that Canberra has in recent years shifted the balance of its attention and resources from an aspirational and outward-looking strategy for multilateral region-building, to a more pessimistic and defensive posture disproportionately focused on Australia's Pacific "inner ring."

The government's signature foreign policy initiative since 2018—the Pacific Step-up—is designed to maintain Australia's coveted role as the partner of choice for economic, development, and security cooperation in its Pacific near abroad. It comes in direct response to China's economic and political overtures to several Pacific island states.

The trouble is that an Australian step-up in the South Pacific also looks suspiciously like a step back in Southeast Asia. One of the most visible manifestations of Canberra's shift in priorities has been to redirect a significant proportion of its annual overseas development assistance from Asia to the South Pacific, a region with a vastly smaller population and far less significance for regional order.

A dozen Pacific island states, with a combined population of eleven million people, now receive more Australian development assistance than all of developing Asia (Figure 4-1).[9] Similarly, the government's answer to China's Belt and Road Initiative—the $2 billion AUD Australian Infrastructure Financing Facility for the Pacific—has been restricted to only financing projects in Pacific island countries and Timor-Leste.[10]

This has been to the detriment of Australia's interests and objectives in its Southeast Asian "middle ring." Absent a more tailored engagement strategy for Southeast Asia—comparable in resourcing to the Pacific Step-up—there are reasons to doubt initiatives based on drawing key Southeast Asian partners closer into Australia's "outer-ring" Indo-Pacific defense partnerships will work.

Australia's regional partners, Indonesia foremost among them, are comfortable, and may even be quietly supportive, of efforts to forge a military balance of power to dilute and constrain Chinese power. However, with the possible exception of Vietnam, they will likely continue to see themselves as distinct from it.

To prevent a hollowing out of its Indo-Pacific strategy, Australia will have to reengage the middle powers of Southeast Asia on their own terms, as well as look for ways to bridge strategic priorities in its two closest geographic theaters.

AUSTRALIA IN THE POST-COVID WORLD

The spread of the coronavirus virus has accelerated existing geopolitical trends—including a near complete breakdown in Australia-China relations.[11] Prime Minister Scott Morrison has likened an "almost irreversible" deterioration in Australia's external outlook to "the existential threat we faced when the global and regional order collapsed in the 1930s and 1940s."[12] With this grim outlook in mind, the government has earmarked $270 billion AUD in defense spending over the next decade. The 2020 Defence Strategic Update calls for new capabilities, including long-range missiles, to enhance Australia's ability to project power and deter adversaries.[13]

The Defence Strategic Update also commits Australia to shaping its strategic environment, broadly defined, from the northeastern Indian Ocean through Southeast Asia to the South Pacific. The emphasis placed on "shaping" all three theaters of Australia's Indo-Pacific strategy sounds

FIGURE 4-1. **Australian's Official Development Assistance**
(ODA) allocations, 2014–2015 vs. 2019–2020

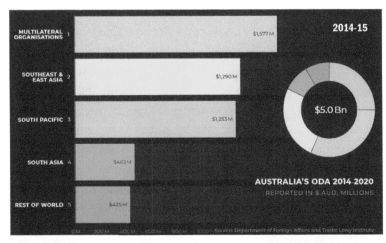

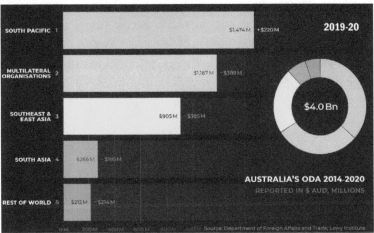

Note: 2019–2020 data shows allocations at beginning of fiscal year, not confirmed expenditures.

Source: "Australian Engagement with Developing Countries: Official Sector Statistical Summary 2014–15" (Canberra: Australian Department of Foreign Affairs and Trade, 2016), 5–6, https://www.dfat.gov.au/sites/default/files/statistical-summary-2014-15.pdf; "Australian Aid Budget Summary 2019–20" (Canberra: Australian Department of Foreign Affairs and Trade, 2019), 7–8, https://www.dfat.gov.au/sites/default/files/2019-20-australian-aid-budget-summary.pdf; "Asia Power Index," Lowy Institute.

obvious, but it is significant. It can be read as a rejection both of outright resignation that the regional order is beyond repair, and of the continentalist strain in Australia's strategic thinking that prioritizes the defense of the country's Pacific approaches.

At issue then is not the stated objective of the Defence Strategic Update, or indeed stepped-up efforts to prepare for a worst-case scenario, but wider failures of omission in Australia's post-COVID strategy. If the aim is to improve—and not just defend against—a disorderly Indo-Pacific, that is the work of creative foreign policy. In focusing on all too evident dangers, we risk overlooking or underestimating opportunities for ambitious regional diplomacy.

Nowhere is Australian diplomacy more consequential than in the "middle ring" of the Indo-Pacific. Australians share a greater overlap of geographically derived interests with the more proximate middle powers of Southeast Asia than they do with any of the Indo-Pacific major powers; whether Japan, India, or the United States. Forging constructive ties with its Southeast Asian neighbors—to bolster their resilience and the Indo-Pacific's rules-based architecture—is among Australia's most pressing priorities. And yet underinvestment in the region and misaligned expectations have complicated this objective.

SOUTHEAST ASIAN CONCERNS

The high-water mark of Australia's Southeast Asian multilateralism came in March 2018, when then Prime Minister Malcolm Turnbull hosted nine of his Southeast Asian counterparts at a special summit in Sydney, the first ASEAN gathering on Australian soil. The optimism surrounding the summit even led to calls in policy circles for Australia to join ASEAN outright, with proponents arguing membership would provide a logical culmination to Australia's decades-long quest to integrate itself with Asia.[14]

Such advocacy—which has never been official government policy—is nevertheless revealing of a dialogue partnership that has often been prone to misplaced hopes, followed by bouts of disappointment.[15] Leaving aside the fact that the ASEAN Charter rules out potential member states not located "in the recognised geographical region of Southeast Asia,"[16] it is highly unlikely there would ever be internal ASEAN support, let alone the consensus required, for bringing Australia into the club.[17]

Perhaps all too predictably, the warm afterglow of the Sydney summit did not last long. Instead, geopolitical pressures have led to a significant—if rarely openly acknowledged—cooling of relations between Australia and the ASEAN grouping since 2018.

Less than eight months after the special ASEAN summit Down Under, a different Australian prime minister, Scott Morrison, announced in November 2018 that Australia was "returning the Pacific to where it should be—front and centre of Australia's strategic outlook."[18] Concerns that the Pacific Step-up has come at the cost of Australia's commitment to Southeast Asia have been raised by senior policy analysts from the region. Liew Chin Tong, an Australian National University graduate who recently served as Malaysia's Deputy Defence Minister, has written for example: "I often wonder nowadays where Australia's Asia dream has gone. At one point, Australia was pushing hard to be considered a part of Asia. That ambition is disappearing."[19]

CHINA: THE ELEPHANT IN THE ROOM

Australia's Pacific Step-up has also highlighted how Australia's relationship with China has shifted to a more adversarial posture. Whereas ASEAN member states are inclined to view U.S.-China rivalry as the main driver of regional instability, for Canberra, President Xi Jinping's China now unequivocally poses the greatest threat to regional and Australian security. ASEAN is often dismissed in this context as an increasingly inadequate and anachronistic mechanism for navigating widening geopolitical fault lines—particularly in the South China Sea.

The mutual apprehension at play here is aptly summed up by the contrasting assessments of two seasoned regional strategists. According to Peter Varghese, the former secretary of Australia's Department of Foreign Affairs and Trade, "ASEAN as a grouping may remain on the sidelines of the strategic balance. But, with some notable exceptions, more and more individual ASEAN nations are being pulled into China's orbit."[20] His former Singaporean counterpart, Bilahari Kausikan, sums up the countervailing view. Of all regional middle powers, in his assessment, "Australia seems the most discombobulated by the new situation, swinging from a position of naive complacency toward China, to one of near-hostility toward all things Chinese."[21]

There is in fact truth in both these statements. ASEAN and its member states are collectively ill-suited to dealing with growing regional security challenges involving China, while Australia's external outlook has become increasingly securitized, less Southeast Asia focused, and more China-driven.

These differences will require concerted effort to manage. It is not enough to say that Australia and its Southeast Asian counterparts share the "lowest common denominator" of interests—stability, security, and prosperity. At the heart of Australia's cooling relations with ASEAN is disagreement about the structure underpinning these goals and the methods used to achieve them.

SHIFT TO MINILATERALISM

Whereas Canberra had once hoped to become more Southeast Asian, through closer integration with ASEAN, today it is banking on its Southeast Asian partners aligning more with Australia's "outer ring" Indo-Pacific diplomacy. Analysts see diminishing marginal returns from closer association with ASEAN-led multilateralism.[22] Instead, Canberra has led the way in proposing variable geometry—bilateral, trilateral, quadrilateral, and "quad plus"—arrangements to carve out alternative security structures that in effect bypass ASEAN.

Progress on "minilateral" initiatives has been remarkable in recent years. Despite a far more modest military capability, Australia is ranked ahead of the United States for its non-allied defense partnerships in the Lowy Institute Asia Power Index.[23] Australia carries less "great power baggage" and has demonstrated it can be far nimbler in Southeast Asia than its U.S. ally.

In August 2018, Indonesia and Australia signed a comprehensive strategic partnership, which includes a pillar on regional stability to enable both sides, in the words of Australia's ambassador to Jakarta, to "shape the Indo-Pacific region in ways we both agree we want it shaped."[24] The following year, Indonesia was instrumental in pushing through the "ASEAN Outlook on the Indo-Pacific"—a symbolically important, if somewhat watered down, regional endorsement of the Indo-Pacific concept. Canberra is also pushing to formalize a "trilateral bloc" with India and Indonesia through joint maritime exercises and consultations between the three sets of foreign and defense ministers.

In late 2019, Morrison visited Hanoi in the first bilateral visit by an Australian leader to Vietnam in twenty-five years. Leaders of the two countries agreed to begin meeting annually, while their defense ministers will also hold yearly exchanges to discuss shared security challenges.[25] Singapore and Australia, meanwhile, have strengthened their comprehensive strategic partnership with a treaty, signed in March 2020, that paves the way for enhanced training deployments for up to 14,000 Singapore Armed Forces (SAF) personnel on annual four-month rotations to Australia.[26] Canberra has also sought to inject new dynamism in its longstanding Five Power Defence Arrangements, which include Malaysia and Singapore.

Australia's comparative advantages as a middle power are evident in these achievements. Nevertheless, they also reveal a growing tendency in Canberra to engage the region primarily through a security lens.

ROADBLOCKS AHEAD

Implicit in Australia's minilateral initiatives is the hope that a narrower grouping of Southeast Asian middle powers will eventually assimilate anxieties about China's role in the region and become net contributors to a broader Indo-Pacific balance of power. Indonesia—on account of its size and geography—is often cited as having great potential to directly support, or at least complement, the Australia-India-Japan-U.S. quadrilateral grouping.[27]

However, expectations that Southeast Asian middle powers will soon join Australia, India, Japan, and the United States in actively counterbalancing China in military and strategic terms have come undone in at least four critical respects:

1. **At a practical level, regional actors lack the heft and physical distance from China required to confront it militarily much outside of their sovereign jurisdictions, and often even from within them.** No Southeast Asian country is particularly suited to participating in a classical concert of powers. Most of the larger players— such as Indonesia, the Philippines, Thailand, and Myanmar—are more concerned about projecting power internally, on unresolved nation-building and security challenges, than they are on project-

ing it externally. The Lowy Institute's Ben Bland, author of the first English-language biography of Indonesian President Joko Widodo, argues "Indonesia's foreign policy is best understood as a reflection of domestic politics, rather than a strategic vision to become a new fulcrum for Asia."[28]

2. **At a political level, there simply remains too profound a disconnect between the Indo-Pacific major powers and even the most strategically minded Southeast Asian players.** Actively balancing China and deterring it from attempts to further alter the status quo in the Indo-Pacific has become the de facto objective framing Canberra's Indo-Pacific strategy.[29] By contrast, Singaporean Prime Minister Lee Hsien Loong has forcefully rejected the reassertion of power politics, notably in his 2019 Shangri-La Dialogue address. The city-state speaks for many smaller actors when it insists it will not take sides but instead will seek to preserve the agency of Southeast Asian middle players amid escalating great power rivalry.[30]

3. **State actors in a region as diverse and historically complex as Southeast Asia are naturally inclined to hedge between powers to manage competing influences.** This is as true of U.S. treaty allies, the Philippines and Thailand, which have become more China-friendly, as it is of communist Vietnam, whose embrace of the West has not ended Hanoi's longstanding party-to-party ties with Beijing. On the other hand, Australia's enduring bonds with the United States effectively rules out an equidistant approach between Washington and Beijing. Morrison has reiterated that the U.S. alliance constitutes "our past, our present, and our future."[31]

4. **Concerns in Southeast Asia about China are not, for the most part, focused on the shifting balance of power at all.** Most countries regard China's rise as inevitable and their dependency on their largest trading partner as something to manage rather than strategically counterbalance. Rather more parochial concerns tend to drive China engagement or pushback, including renegotiating infrastructure loan agreements, sensitivities around diaspora communities, and maritime boundary disputes.

The dilemma this poses Canberra is that the same impediments that dis-enamoured ASEAN in the eyes of Australian policymakers also exist in Australia's bilateral relationships with individual Southeast Asian partners. The problems arise not from ASEAN itself—which as an institution is often less than the sum of its parts—but rather from the characteristics of its member states.

A failure to recognize, or the urge to gloss over, these realities will likely result in disappointment. What is needed from Canberra is a more tailored approach to working with the middle powers of Southeast Asia—one that takes greater stock of their development needs, and is not exclusively couched in terms of competition with China.

OPPORTUNITIES IN A POST-COVID WORLD

The onset of COVID-19 presents a significant inflection point in Australia's relationship with the region. Governments and societies, almost without exception, are facing a toxic mix of public health, economic, security, and strategic challenges. The Morrison government has been blunt in its appraisal, outlining "a post-COVID world that is poorer, that is more dangerous, and that is more disorderly."[32]

Nevertheless, Australia's strategic circumstances, while critical, are also dynamic. They create an opportunity to rethink, reorder, and step up Canberra's Southeast Asia engagement. Importantly, the pandemic allows for a more precise articulation of Australia's shared interests with the middle players of Southeast Asia.

According to the ISEAS State of Southeast Asia survey in 2020, Japan is regarded as the most trusted major power among Southeast Asians policymakers, with 61.2% of respondents expressing confidence in Tokyo to "do the right thing" in providing global public goods, in contrast to 30.3 and 16.1% for the United States and China, respectively.[33]

Japan's regional standing and willingness to invest in Southeast Asia's development for its own sake underscores the importance for Australia of being a trusted, committed, and respected development partner for the region. This can only strengthen Australia's engagement on the merits of a balance of power that seeks to uphold the regional rules-based order.

Helping the region to sustainably recover from the pandemic will require improving health security, alleviating poverty and inequality, strengthening domestic and multilateral institutions, and shoring up the international trading system. To do so, Australia will have to invest not only in defense partnerships, but in its development and economic tools of statecraft.

A SOUTHEAST ASIA STEP-UP

Southeast Asian governments, understandably, are far more concerned by the domestic crises confronting them than the pandemic's geopolitical implications. The ability of authorities to manage the myriad secondary consequences of the pandemic—including falling demand for exports, the emergence of a new class of "COVID-poor," and lost government revenues—is being severely tested.[34] Yet stalled recoveries and state weakness in Southeast Asia would have unavoidable implications for the regional balance of power—with detrimental consequences for Australia's future security and prosperity.

At the same time, neither the United States nor China appears presently able to mount a credible international response. That leaves an opening for a networked grid of "competent powers" to lead regional recovery efforts.[35]

Australia is set to be among the first to onshore manufacturing of one, or more, of the first successful COVID-19 vaccines. Canberra has committed $80 million AUD to the World Health Organization's global COVAX initiative for the equitable global distribution of coronavirus vaccines. Plans are underway for the Australian Indo-Pacific Centre for Health Security to assist in rolling out coronavirus vaccines to the Pacific island states, Indonesia, Cambodia, Laos, Myanmar, the Philippines, and Vietnam.[36]

This initiative marks a significant first step in bridging the needs of the two Indo-Pacific theaters of greatest concern to Canberra. However, if Australia wants to have a role in shaping the long-term trajectory of Southeast Asia, it will require a level of engagement comparable in scale and breadth to the Pacific Step-up. An Australian post-COVID aid strategy could be enhanced through a consortium of trusted actors—including Japan and the European Union—jointly committing to a roadmap for Southeast Asia's recovery.

Enhanced Australian development assistance should aim ultimately not only to improve regional health security but to help the most vulnerable countries—particularly those in Mekong Southeast Asia—become more resilient, effective, and equitable countries. This would put them in a better position to withstand direct and indirect interference in their body politics from China. In many ways, the skills and expertise needed for a multiyear regional recovery effort—whether in healthcare, education, or capacity building—would also play more directly to Australia's strengths than attempts to compete with China on infrastructure financing.

MULTILATERAL REBOOT

Finally, Australia should rediscover its confidence as a middle power that looks to the positives and potential of Southeast Asian multilateralism in the wake of the pandemic. Balancing minilateral and multilateral diplomacy requires a clearer differentiation of objectives, between deterring China through strategic partnerships, on one hand, and cooperating with a more diverse set of middle powers in shoring up the rules-based regional order, on the other. Both approaches will ultimately reinforce each other in creating strategic balance to offset China's growing power in the Indo-Pacific.

The government has been right to migrate its defense diplomacy to minilaterals in response to intramural ASEAN divisions on regional security challenges. It is true a one-size-fits-all ASEAN approach to external strategic balancing will not work. However, neither should ASEAN's ability to keep the peace among ten very different countries be underestimated or taken for granted.

The "ASEAN way" still offers Australia a critical if underappreciated security dividend. Consensus-based decision making, while slow and often aspirational, nevertheless functions as a safeguard against the recurrence of great power proxy conflicts that destabilized the region during the Cold War. As the principle comes under greater strain, paradoxically it also takes on greater significance.

AN ECONOMIC BALANCE OF POWER

For all its flaws, ASEAN-centered multilateral architecture also continues to provide the only viable, broad-based, and suitably nonaligned alternative to a Sino-centric order in the Indo-Pacific. The goal then should be to help Southeast Asian countries maintain regional balance in the ways they do best: by slowly weaving together a set of rules among diverse actors for the region's economic governance.

What the quadrilateral grouping delivers for the military balance of power in the Indo-Pacific, ASEAN can deliver for the regional economic balance of power. ASEAN's support for the Comprehensive and Progressive Agreement for Trans-Pacific Partnership, which came into effect without the United States at the end of 2018, and its progress toward the Regional Comprehensive Economic Partnership (RCEP), despite India's withdrawal in 2020, are examples of the region's commitment to strengthening the economic rules-based order.

The success of homegrown multilateral initiatives—often in spite of the protectionist and decoupling agendas of major Indo-Pacific powers—will not only be crucial for post-COVID recovery efforts but ultimately offers the most compelling answer to Beijing's preference for bilateral economic diplomacy, as seen in the Belt and Road Initiative. The lowering of trade barriers under RCEP between developed economies—Australia, Japan, and South Korea—and large developing economies—such as Indonesia and Vietnam—can help to build a multilateral hedge to China's asymmetric economic power.

In so doing, ASEAN proves three things. First, a broad church of middle players can still forge a pan-regional consensus on important components of the rules-based order, despite their diversity of interests and alignments. Second, China's power, while significant, is not yet so severe that it must subsume all the interests of its neighborhood. Third, ASEAN-centered diplomacy can still bind Beijing to multilateral modes of regional governance when it has strength in numbers.

BRIDGING AUSTRALIA'S INDO-PACIFIC THEATERS

The same lessons may well extend to Australia's Pacific "inner ring." China's expanding economic clout means Australia's strategic theaters are inevitably merging. To succeed in its Indo-Pacific strategy, Canberra will have to actively seek to bridge distinct geopolitical games.

The developing economies of the South Pacific—notably the largest, Papua New Guinea and Fiji—increasingly look to Asia as a source of inward investment and deepening trade. Without acknowledging and facilitating the aspirations of Pacific countries to want to connect with Asia, China's overtures may only find greater traction in the region.

Canberra, however, is uniquely placed to facilitate and deepen cross-regional linkages between Southeast Asia and the South Pacific. This can be done by exploring a variety of opportunities:

1. The Australian Infrastructure Financing Facility should aim more explicitly to integrate the Pacific island states with the economic hubs of Southeast Asia via interregional transport and connectivity projects.

2. As the intergovernmental organizations in their respective regions, ASEAN and the Pacific Islands Forum (PIF)—a grouping of eighteen countries and territories, of which Australia is the largest—could be encouraged to institutionalize economic cooperation between their member states.

3. Australia should invite a broad grouping of Pacific island states to participate on the sidelines of biennial ASEAN-Australia summits, providing an opportunity for Pacific island leaders to engage directly with their Southeast Asian counterparts.

4. Canberra could also lobby for Papua New Guinea, the second-largest of the PIF states and a country that sits on the geographic continuum of Southeast Asia, to become an annual participant at the East Asia Summit.

Bringing Australia's Pacific neighborhood into contact with Southeast Asia's big-tent diplomacy would help to diversify the international relations of the Pacific island states, socialize their leaders into wider discussions on regional order, encourage agency and minimize the risk that these smaller players are treated as pawns in great power rivalry.

For Australia and its Southeast Asian partners alike, these initiatives would reaffirm the relevance of cooperative regionalism at the core of any durable Indo-Pacific balance of power.

Notes

1. "2017 Foreign Policy White Paper" (Canberra: Australian Department of Foreign Affairs and Trade, November 2017), 3, https://www.dfat.gov.au/sites/default /files/2017-foreign-policy-white-paper.pdf.

2. Bruce Hunt, *Australia's Northern Shield? Papua New Guinea and the Defence of Australia since 1880* (Melbourne: Monash University Publishing, 2017).

3. The idea of three concentric circles of Australian strategic interests is loosely based on Andrew Carr's distinction of an Australian "inner-ring" of core interests and an "outer-ring" encompassing the Indo-Pacific and the wider world. See Andrew Carr, "No Longer a Middle Power: Australia's Strategy in the 21st Century" (Paris: IFRI, September 2019), https://www.ifri.org/en/publications/etudes-de-lifri/focus -strategique/no-longer-middle-power-australias-strategy-21st.

4. Ibid, 28.

5. "2017 Foreign Policy White Paper," Australian Department of Foreign Affairs and Trade, 43.

6. Rory Medcalf, *Contest for the Indo-Pacific: Why China Won't Map the Future* (Melbourne: La Trobe University Press, March 2020).

7. "Asia Power Index: 2020 Edition," Lowy Institute, 2020, https://power. lowyinstitute.org/.

8. "2016 Defence White Paper" (Canberra: Australian Department of Defence, February 2016), 70, https://www.defence.gov.au/whitepaper/docs/2016-defence -white-paper.pdf.

9. "Australian Aid Budget at a Glance 2019-20" (Canberra: Australian Department of Foreign Affairs and Trade, 2019), https://www.dfat.gov.au/sites/default/files /2019-20-aus-aid-budget-at-a-glance.pdf.

10. "About," Australian Infrastructure Financing Facility for the Pacific, https:// www.aiffp.gov.au/about.

11. Natasha Kassam, "Great expectations: The unravelling of the Australia -China relationship" (Washington, DC: The Brookings Institution, July 20, 2020), https://www.brookings.edu/articles/great-expectations-the-unraveling-of-the -australia-china-relationship/.

12. Scott Morrison, "Address: Launch of the 2020 Defence Strategic Update" (speech, Canberra, July 1, 2020), https://www.pm.gov.au/media/address-launch -2020-defence-strategic-update.

13. "Force Structure Plan 2020" (Canberra: Australian Department of Defense, July 2020), 36, https://www.defence.gov.au/StrategicUpdate-2020/docs/2020_Force _Structure_Plan.pdf.

14. See for example Graeme Dobell, "Australia as an ASEAN Community partner" (Barton, Australia: Australian Strategic Policy Institute, February 2018), https://www.aspi.org.au/report/australia-asean-community-partner.

15. This is not a new phenomenon. See for example Rhondda M. Nicholas, "Misperception and Muddled Thinking in Australia-ASEAN Relations," *Contemporary Southeast Asia* 5, no. 2 (September 1983): 153–71, http://www.jstor.org/stable /25797756.

16. "The ASEAN Charter" (Jakarta: ASEAN Secretariat, January 2008), https://asean.org/wp-content/uploads/images/archive/publications/ASEAN-Charter.pdf.

17. Malcolm Cook, "ASEAN-Australia Relations: The suitable status quo" (Sydney: Lowy Institute, August 2018), https://www.lowyinstitute.org/publications/asean-australia-relations-suitable-status-quo.

18. Scott Morrison, "Australia and the Pacific: A New Chapter" (speech, Townsville, Australia, November 8, 2018), https://www.pm.gov.au/media/address-australia-and-pacific-new-chapter.

19. Chin Tong Liew, "Towards a peaceful and inclusive Asia," Lowy Institute, October 30, 2019, https://www.lowyinstitute.org/the-interpreter/towards-peaceful-and-inclusive-asia.

20. Peter Varghese, "Constructing a New Strategic Equilibrium in the Indo-Pacific," Australian Strategic Policy Institute, June 21, 2019, https://www.aspistrategist.org.au/constructing-a-new-strategic-equilibrium-in-the-indo-pacific/.

21. Bilahari Kausikan, "How Indo-Pacific Countries Can Keep their Options Open," *Nikkei Asia*, August 22, 2020, https://asia.nikkei.com/Opinion/How-Indo-Pacific-countries-can-keep-their-options-open.

22. Euan Graham, "Is ASEAN still central to Australia?," Lowy Institute, February 5, 2019, https://www.lowyinstitute.org/the-interpreter/asean-still-central-australia.

23. "Asia Power Index," Lowy Institute.

24. Gary Quinlan, "Australia and Indonesia: Speech to the Jakarta Foreign Correspondents Club" (speech, Jakarta, November 27, 2019), https://indonesia.embassy.gov.au/jakt/AR19_003.html.

25. "Joint Statement between Viet Nam and Australia," Prime Minister of Australia, August 23, 2019, https://www.pm.gov.au/media/joint-statement-between-viet-nam-and-australia.

26. "Australia-Singapore Military Training Initiative: Treaty on Military Training and Training Area Development" (Canberra: Australian Department of Defense, March 23, 2020), https://www.defence.gov.au/Initiatives/ASMTI/News/2020-03-23-Treaty-on-Military-Training.asp.

27. See for example Andrew Tillett and Emma Connors, "New bloc of Australia, India, Indonesia takes shape amid China fears," *Australian Financial Review*, September 4, 2020, https://www.afr.com/politics/federal/new-bloc-of-australia-india-indonesia-takes-shape-amid-china-fears-20200904-p55sec.

28. Ben Bland, *Man of Contradictions: Joko Widodo and the struggle to remake Indonesia* (Sydney: Penguin Books Australia, September 2020), 137.

29. While China is rarely named directly, it is clear the government has China in mind when the prime minister refers to Australia holding "potential adversaries, forces, and infrastructure at risk from greater distance and therefore influence their calculus of costs involved in threatening Australia's interests." See Scott Morrison, "Address: Launch of the 2020 Defence Strategic Update."

30. Lee Hsien Loong, "Keynote Address at the 2019 Shangri-La Dialogue" (speech, Singapore, May 31, 2019), https://www.pmo.gov.sg/Newsroom/PM-Lee-Hsien-Loong-at-the-IISS-Shangri-La-Dialogue-2019.

31. Scott Morrison, "Lowy Lecture 'In our Interest,'" (speech, Sydney, October 3, 2019), https://www.pm.gov.au/media/speech-lowy-lecture-our-interest.

32. Scott Morrison, "Address: Launch of the 2020 Defence Strategic Update."

33. Tang Siew Mun, Hoang Thi Ha, Anuthida Saelaow Qian, Glenn Ong, and Pham Thi Phuong Thao, "The State of Southeast Asia: 2020 Survey Report" (Singapore: ISEAS-Yusof Ishak Institute, January 2020), https://www.iseas.edu.sg/wp-content/uploads/pdfs/TheStateofSEASurveyReport_2020.pdf.

34. Gwen Robinson, "Coronavirus pushes 38m Asians below poverty line: World Bank," *Nikkei Asia*, September 29, 2020, https://asia.nikkei.com/Economy/Coronavirus-pushes-38m-Asians-below-poverty-line-World-Bank.

35. Michael Fullilove, "Coronavirus: Global giants stumble while agile nations inspire," *The Australian*, April 6, 2020, https://www.lowyinstitute.org/publications/coronavirus-global-giants-stumble-while-agile-nations-inspire.

36. "Australia to promote COVID-19 vaccine equity for developing countries," Indo-Pacific Centre for Health Security, Australian Government, https://indopacifichealthsecurity.dfat.gov.au/australia-promote-covid-19-vaccine-equity-developing-countries.

5

China and the West Competing Over Infrastructure in Southeast Asia

DAVID DOLLAR

INTRODUCTION

The United States and China are promoting competing economic programs in Southeast Asia. China got in first, when President Xi Jinping of China proposed the Belt and Road Initiative (BRI) in a pair of speeches in 2013. In Kazakhstan, he outlined a vision of restoring overland trade routes from China to Central Asia and Europe—the ancient "Silk Road." In Indonesia, he introduced the concept of a "Maritime Silk Road," which is essentially the already well-traveled sea corridor south from China through the South China Sea and the Indian Ocean, on to the Middle East and Europe. While part of the Chinese effort on BRI is aimed at these specific corridors, the program is in fact global and not directed at any specific geography. Latin America is deeply involved, as are all parts of Africa. The main objective is for China to lend money to developing countries to construct infrastructure in transport, power, water supply, and other sectors. In his opening remarks at the Belt and Road Forum in Beijing in May 2017, President Xi noted that:

Infrastructure connectivity is the foundation of development through cooperation. We should promote land, maritime, air and cyberspace connectivity, concentrate our efforts on key passageways, cities and projects and connect networks of highways, railways and sea ports...We need to seize opportunities presented by the new round of change in energy mix and the revolution in energy technologies to develop global energy interconnection and achieve green and low-carbon development. We should improve trans-regional logistics network and promote connectivity of policies, rules and standards so as to provide institutional safeguards for enhancing connectivity.[1]

The initiative is generally popular in the developing world, where almost all countries face infrastructure deficiencies. According to the Chinese government, 125 countries have signed onto the BRI as of April 2019, including all 10 ASEAN countries.

While the initiative is popular with developing countries, it has received various criticisms from the leaders of advanced industrial economies. One valid criticism is that the program lacks transparency, so it is difficult to find details on how much China is lending for different projects, what the terms of the loans are, how contractors were chosen, and what environmental and social risks are involved. Horn, Reinhart, and Trebesch find that much of China's overseas lending does not appear in the World Bank and International Monetary Fund (IMF) data for sovereign debt.[2] BRI has also been criticized as an effort to export China's authoritarian model, as a number of major loan recipients have poor records of democracy and civil liberties (for example, Venezuela in Latin America, Cambodia and Laos in Asia, and Sudan and Zimbabwe in Africa). While the advanced economies have generally been critical of the initiative, Italy broke ranks with the rest of the G-7 and signed up for BRI in 2019.

U.S. opposition to China's initiative is crystalized in the Trump administration's Free and Open Indo-Pacific (FOIP) program. According to Stromseth, "FOIP singles out China for pursuing regional hegemony, says Beijing is leveraging 'predatory economics' to coerce other nations, and poses a clear choice between 'free' and 'repressive' visions of world order in the Indo-Pacific region."[3]

The objective of this chapter is to examine the competing U.S. and Chinese initiatives in the area of infrastructure in Southeast Asia in light of available information and to combat common misconceptions and unsubstantiated rhetoric. The next section focuses on infrastructure needs and the existing track record of Western assistance. The third section of the chapter then focuses on the implementation of China's BRI in ASEAN countries.

INFRASTRUCTURE NEEDS AND WESTERN ASSISTANCE

Investing in infrastructure is a crucial aspect of a successful growth strategy. McKinsey takes stock of infrastructure investment in all countries of the world and concludes that there is a significant gap between what countries are spending and their infrastructure requirements if they are to continue to grow well until 2035.[4] Emerging Asia, excluding China and India—which would mostly be ASEAN—could productively spend $300 billion per year on infrastructure. The big-ticket items are transport and power, with significant needs in water supply and sanitation as well. Most of these resources need to come from domestic savings, and many countries are already investing significantly in infrastructure. Indonesia, for example, is implementing 75% of the needed investment. But on the other hand, that means that 25% of infrastructure requirements go unmet. In general, the developing world will have to finance or attract more infrastructure investment if it is to meet its growth objectives.

Traditionally, ASEAN countries could rely on Western support—through bilateral financing and the multilateral development banks—to finance some of their infrastructure investment. However, that is no longer the case. Japan is the only significant financier of infrastructure remaining. During 2015–2017, Japan committed $13 billion to transport and energy infrastructure in ASEAN countries. No other Western donor reached $1 billion per year. The total from the six major Western sources—Australia, Japan, Asian Development Bank (ADB), World Bank, United States, and South Korea—amounted to about 2% of infrastructure financing needs for the ASEAN countries.[5] Two things are going on here. First, the overall amount of Western aid is not keeping up with needs. Second, the donors are generally turning away from infrastructure. When initially set up, 70% of World Bank financing went to infrastructure. During 2015–2017, only 29% of World Bank support to ASEAN went to infrastructure. The figure for ADB was only slightly better at 39%.

The multilateral development banks have tied themselves up in com-plicated environmental and social safeguards such that doing large infra-structure projects with them is time-consuming and expensive.[6] The result is that little infrastructure is financed.

The U.S.-led FOIP program initially had little economic content and fo-cused more on security issues. However, this changed with the Better Utili-zation of Investment Leading to Development (BUILD) Act, signed into law in October 2018, which establishes a new U.S. International Development Finance Corporation and doubles U.S. development finance capacity to $60 billion worldwide. Additionally, the U.S. Overseas Private Investment Cor-poration (OPIC) signed a Memorandum of Understanding (MOU) with the development finance agencies of Japan and Australia to "catalyze Indo-Pacific investment projects that produce quality infrastructure, increase connectivity, and promote sustainable economic growth."[7] The three coun-tries have picked a $1 billion liquified natural gas project in Papua New Guinea as their first case for joint financing under the MOU. They plan to abide by the Group of 20 (G-20) principles for "quality infrastructure invest-

FIGURE 5-1. FDI Restrictiveness Index for Power Generation, Power Distribution, and Transport, 2018 (0=Open; 1=Closed)

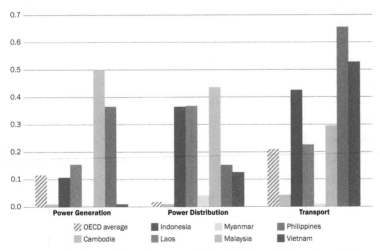

Source: The OECD, FDI Regulatory Restrictive Index 2018, https://qdd.oecd.org/subject.aspx? Subject=ASEAN_INDEX.

ment," adopted at the G-20 summit in Osaka in June 2019, and sent a joint delegation to Indonesia in August to explore other potential projects.

Another aspect of declining Western support for infrastructure is the ideological view that infrastructure can be left to private investment. This is certainly true in telecom, but in transport and power it has proved hard to attract private investment. Partly the problem is regulatory restrictions in developing countries. The OECD calculates an FDI restrictiveness index for different sectors. In transport and power generation and distribution, ASEAN countries tend to be more restrictive than OECD countries. However, countries that are very open such as Cambodia or Myanmar still struggle to attract private participation in infrastructure. This is an area where countries need capacity building support in order to intelligently open their sectors and to manage the complex contracts that are typical in infrastructure.

CHINA'S INFRASTRUCTURE FINANCING IN SOUTHEAST ASIA

It is difficult to say how much Chinese financing is going to infrastructure in Southeast Asia because the Chinese effort lacks transparency. China's loans are largely coming from the two policy banks: China Development Bank and China EXIM Bank. They borrow on domestic and international capital markets and lend with a spread, so they expect to be financially self-sufficient. EXIM has access to some subsidies from the Ministry of Finance so that some of its lending can be concessional. The motivation for China is partly economic; the economy has excess savings and underemployed construction companies and heavy industry. The projects are a way to put these resources to use. Also, if infrastructure is improved in developing countries, then China—as well as other countries—will benefit indirectly as trade expands. A 2019 World Bank study estimates that there would be very significant gains to the recipient countries from the transport projects in BRI, as well as spillover benefits to China and the rest of the world. The study also notes that in many countries, poor policies are more of an impediment than poor infrastructure.[8] There is also strategic motivation as China gains friends and influence through these projects. A further strategic consideration is that China would like to have alternate routes to transport natural resources, routes that are not controlled by the United States and its allies.

While it is hard to get reliable data on Chinese lending for infrastructure, an academic exercise under the name AidData has put together estimates of Chinese lending to different countries and sectors through 2014.[9] Working with those data, I showed that China's lending was indiscriminate in terms of geography and governance. That is, the lending is not aimed at the BRI corridors but rather is a global endeavor, and the countries receiving loans have very different governance.[10] Three of the top twenty borrowers according to these data were ASEAN countries: Cambodia, Indonesia, and Laos. They illustrated the point about governance as Indonesia is a democratic country, whereas Cambodia and Laos are authoritarian. Based on the amounts lent to those three countries, it seems likely that China's lending is of the same scale as Japan's lending.

Table 5-1 lists major projects in ASEAN countries undertaken with Chinese financing since 2015. The list is not exhaustive and has been developed from press reports. The projects include coal-fired power in Indonesia and hydro in Laos. Major transport projects involve rail in Malaysia, Laos, and Indonesia, and road expansion in Cambodia, Laos, and Indonesia. Most of the loans are on commercial terms, in dollars at flexible interest rates. Some are concessional, such as the loan to Cambodia for urban roads.

Since China's money is mostly not concessional, it has been accused of

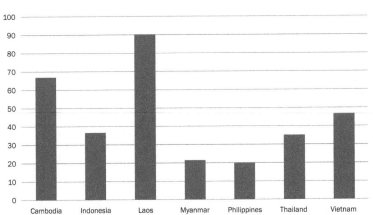

FIGURE 5-2. **External Debt, 2018 (% of GNI)**

Source: The World Bank, World Development Indicators 2017, http://databank.worldbank.org/data/reports.aspx?source=world-development-indicators.

TABLE 5-1. Some Major Infrastructure Projects Funded by China, 2015–Present

Country	Loan (USD Millions)	Financier	Year	Sector	Project	Details
Cambodia	$351	EXIM	2018	Transport	—	The concessional loan agreement was signed on July 10 between the Export-Import Bank of China and Cambodia's Ministry of Finance to build a four-lane, 47-kilometre city ring road.
Indonesia	$125	AIIB	2017	Multi-Sector	Dam Operational Improvement and Safety Project Phase II	The Project Objectives are to increase the safety and functionality of existing dams in selected locations and strengthen the operation and management capacity for dam safety.
Indonesia	$270	China EXIM Bank; Industrial and Commercial Bank of China (ICBC)	2016	Energy	Coal-fired plant in Bengkulu	China-invested power plant starts construction in Indonesia to resolve electricity shortage.
Indonesia	$3,000	China Development Bank (CDB)	2016	Infrastructure	Infrastructure Construction	China Development Bank has issued $3 billion 10-year loans to three Indonisian banks (Bank Negara Indonesia, Bank Rakyat Indonesia and Bank Mandiri) for infrastructure construction in the Southeast Asian country.
Indonesia	$4,500	CDB	2015	Transport	Jakarta-Bandung High-Speed Rail	The Jakarta-Bandung high-speed railway will span 142 kilometers (88 miles) when complete, and is expected to cut the journey between the two cities from the current three to five hours down to 45 minutes.
Laos	$40	AIIB	2019	Transport	National Road 13 Improvement and Maintenance Project	This is AIIB's first approved project in Lao PDR. 58 kilometers of road will be rehabilitated in order to improve functionality, safety and climate resilience.
Laos	$600	EXIM	2016	Energy	Nam Ngum 4 Hydroelectric Power Project	The project will maximise the efficiency of the Nam Ngum River's hydropower cascade development and boost national foreign exchange reserves.
Laos	The cost of the project is estimated at $5.95 billion, of which 12 percent are financed by Laos directly, 28 percent by China and the remaining 60 percent by loans from Chinese banks.	—	2015	Transport	Vientane-Boten Railway	The 414-km China-Laos Railway runs from Boten, the northern Lao town bordering the south-western Chinese province of Yunnan, to Vientiane, capital of Laos, with an operating speed of 160km/h. The electrified passenger and cargo railway, on which construction started in December 2016 with the full application of Chinese management and technical standards, is scheduled to be completed and open to traffic in December 2021.
Malaysia	85% of the total cost (~$8bn)	EXIM	2016	Transport	East Coast Railway Link	The rail link is meant to connect much of Peninsular Malaysia's eastern coast, whose economy lags the wealthier western coast, to a major port near Kuala Lumpur. The project was suspended due to the ballooned cost, but was resumed in April 2019 as China Communications Construction Co. and Malaysia Rail Link Sdn signed a supplementary agreement for the reduced cost.
Myanmar	$20	Asian Infrastructure Investment Bank (AIIB)	2016	Energy	Myingyan 225 MW Combined Cycle Gas Turbine (CCGT) Power Plant Project, Myanmar	The AIIB is providing US$270 million of debt financing for the development, construction, and operation of a greenfield 225 MW Combined Cycle Gas Turbine (CCGT) power plant in the Mandalay region of Myanmar.

"debt trap diplomacy"—that is, of saddling countries with high-interest debt that they are unable to repay, giving China leverage over the borrowing country. External debt is different from domestic debt in that it ultimately has to be serviced by exports, so there is a limit to how much debt a country can take on without putting itself at risk of a financial and balance of payments crisis. In a speech in May 2019, Secretary of State Mike Pompeo criticized China for peddling "corrupt infrastructure deals in exchange for political influence," and using "bribe-fueled debt-trap diplomacy" to undermine good governance.[11]

Looking at the data on external debt relative to GNI for ASEAN countries, most of them are in very good financial shape as of 2018, so that debt sustainability is not much of a worry. The exceptions are Laos, with external debt at 90% of GNI, and, to a lesser extent, Cambodia (68%). Hurley, Morris, and Portelance assess the likelihood of debt problems in 68 countries along the land and maritime transport corridors. They find that 8 out of 68 countries are at risk of debt distress because of borrowing from China, including Laos. They do not see Cambodia having severe risk yet, but its external debt has risen rapidly.[12] Their analysis takes account of future planned projects so that they can look at the trajectory of external debt over the next few years. Hence, debt sustainability is a concern for these smaller economies, but not a big issue for the large economies of ASEAN, which can afford to take on more debt.

To summarize the debt issues for ASEAN countries: Laos highlights the risk of taking on too much debt too quickly, especially nonconcessional debt. According to the IMF, Laos is at high risk of debt distress.[13] As a low-income country, Laos is eligible for the Debt Service Suspension Initiative promoted by the G20. However, Laos has chosen not to participate and instead is negotiating directly with China, its main creditor, including a debt-for-equity swap in which the China Southern Power Grid Co. takes a direct stake in Laos's power transmission company.[14] The other countries of ASEAN are not at risk of debt distress. An important caveat, however, is that not all Chinese lending may be included in the standard data for external debt, as China is not transparent enough about its lending.

While most of China's lending has come from CDB and EXIM, an interesting new development is the Asian Infrastructure Investment Bank (AIIB), launched by China, headquartered in Beijing, and now with 100+ members. Around the time of the Global Financial Crisis, an international commission under the chairmanship of Ernesto Zedillo examined the performance of the World Bank and the other multilateral development banks (MDBs) and made recommendations for modernizing them.[15] This commission had good representation from the developing world (including Zhou Xiaochuan from China) and made a series of practical recommendations: increase the voting shares of developing countries to reflect their growing weight in the world economy, abolish the resident board as an expensive anachronism given modern technology, increase the lending capacity of the MDBs to meet growing developing world needs, re-establish the focus on infrastructure and growth, and streamline the implementation of environmental and social safeguards in order to speed up project implementation.

China generally shared these criticisms of the MDBs. In the wake of the Zedillo report, however, there was no meaningful reform. This frustration with lack of reform in the World Bank, combined with a general dissatisfaction with the U.S.-led global financial system, influenced China to launch the new development bank. Alex He notes: "Indeed, China and other emerging powers have criticized the World Bank and the IMF for their inefficient and over-supervised processes of granting loans. The current gap between the demands for infrastructure investment and available investment from existing international financing organizations in developing countries creates an opportunity for emerging economies to establish a new type of bank with a directed focus in this area."[16]

The charter of the AIIB follows very much in the spirit of the charters of the World Bank and ADB, but also incorporates virtually all of the Zedillo report recommendations: majority ownership by the developing world, no resident board, authority to lend more from a given capital base, a focus on infrastructure and growth, and environmental and social guidelines that should be implemented in proportion to the risk.[17]

The AIIB approved its first project in June 2016. In the three years since, it has approved forty-six projects for a total of $8.5 billion in financing. The projects, listed on its website, are diverse in terms of countries and sectors. Projects in ASEAN include Indonesia slum upgrading, Philippines flood management, and Laos road improvement, to name a few. While the AIIB portfolio covers a diverse group of countries, not surprisingly the largest borrowers tend to be the largest economies in Asia. India is by far the largest borrower, with 27% of the $8.5 billion lent so far. Other large borrowers are Indonesia (11%), Turkey (11%), Bangladesh (7%), and Pakistan (5%).

CONCLUSIONS AND RECOMMENDATIONS

One of the main objectives of this chapter is to make the ASEAN experience with BRI infrastructure projects more real: What infrastructure are these projects building? Which countries are the main borrowers? What are the terms of the loans and how do they fit into the overall government debt management? Are we likely to see a slew of debt crises? Are the countries supported mostly authoritarian ones? Do the borrowing countries have the necessary supporting technologies to connect to global markets? How does the Chinese effort interact with the U.S.-led Free and Open Indo-Pacific initiative?

These are difficult questions to answer definitively, but experience and data are on the increase. The most striking result from this review is the *heterogeneity* of experiences among ASEAN countries. The projects are mostly in transport and power, but are nevertheless diverse: international rail, urban transport, expressways, hydropower, carbon-based power, transmission lines—to name just some. The major borrowing countries are spread out over the world and not confined to the geography of the "Silk Road Economic Belt" and "Maritime Silk Road" as originally laid out by Xi Jinping. Some of these are authoritarian countries, whereas others are more democratic.

The large countries in ASEAN were in good financial shape prior to the coronavirus crisis, so fears of "debt-trap diplomacy" were overblown. The smaller economies—Laos especially—were more at risk. Most worrisome are the loans that are at commercial, flexible interest rates. It is likely that the coronavirus will lead to public health crises in many developing countries, including those in ASEAN. What is even more certain is that the global recession will hit these countries hard. Prices for the primary products that many developing countries export are down substantially, and trade volumes are way off. So, countries will not be able to earn the resources they need to service their debts. The G-20 has endorsed the idea of a debt moratorium on payments by low-income countries. Horn, Reinhart, and Trebesch find at least 140 instances of China restructuring or writing off debts since 2000.[18] So, it is realistic to expect China to participate in a new round of rescheduling and write-offs. While China and the West have been competing over infrastructure in Southeast Asia, coordinating on debt relief will now be an important area for cooperation.

Finally, I would argue that there is some initial evidence that China is learning from its experience and improving its practices. In the early days of Chinese lending to the developing world, Chinese institutions showed little concern for debt sustainability issues. Now the Chinese lending is often captured in IMF programs that have overall borrowing ceilings and that should ensure sustainable build-up of debt. In the case of Malaysia, the major rail project was redesigned and scaled down after a new government came to power and requested changes, an example of pragmatism on the part of the Chinese partners. Russell and Berger similarly find pragmatic adaptation on the part of the Chinese in their Southeast Asian projects.[19]

These results also have implications for how the United States and its Western allies should respond to BRI:

- Dial down the anti-China rhetoric and join AIIB (United States, Japan). U.S. accusations of China's "debt-trap diplomacy" do not resonate with much of the developing world and make the United States seem insecure. AIIB is transparent and multilateral and the United States and Japan should be encouraging the expansion of this effort, as an alternative to Chinese bilateral financing. Joining AIIB would show that the United States and Japan are not simply opposing all Chinese external efforts and would give more credence to Western criticisms of China's bilateral programs.

- Support additional human and financial resources for the IMF as this is the institution that is best placed to help developing countries manage their external borrowing and to integrate Chinese projects into their budget management and development strategies. The world tends to underinvest in the IMF during boom times, leaving it under-resourced when crises hit. The worldwide recession in the wake of the coronavirus will probably usher in a new round of developing country financial crises and the IMF will need to take the lead in limiting the financial and economic toll.

- Encourage the World Bank to focus more on infrastructure and to reduce processing times for its loans, giving developing countries competitive alternatives. This would require the bank to rely more on the environmental and social safeguards that developing countries themselves have in place, rather than creating an expensive super-structure to micro-manage projects. Without more risk-taking it is hard to see how the traditional institutions can compete with Chinese banks or countries' own financing.

- Increase cooperation with long-standing partners, such as Japan, Australia, and Singapore, to support sustainable infrastructure development in Southeast Asia. This should include a focus on capacity building, especially to manage infrastructure projects, both from private investors and from Chinese lenders.

Notes

1. Xi Jinping, "Work Together to Build the Silk Road Economic Belt and The 21st Century Maritime Silk Road" (speech, Beijing, China, May 14, 2017), http://news.xinhuanet.com/english/2017-05/14/c_136282982.htm.

2. Sebastian Horn, Carmen Reinhart, and Christoph Trebesch, "China's Overseas Lending," Working Paper 26050 (Cambridge, Mass.: National Bureau of Economic Research, July 2019).

3. Jonathan Stromseth, "Don't Make Us Choose: Southeast Asia in the throes of U.S.-China Rivalry" (Washington, D.C.: The Brookings Institution, October 2019), www.brookings.edu/research/dont-make-us-choose-southeast-asia-in-the-throes-of-us-china-rivalry/.

4. Jonathan Woetzel, Nicklas Garemo, Jan Mischke, Priyanka Kamra, and Robert Palter, "Bridging Infrastructure Gaps: Has the World Made Progress?" (Washington, D.C., McKinsey Global Institute, October 2017), www.mckinsey.com/industries/capital-projects-and-infrastructure/our-insights/bridging-infrastructure-gaps-has-the-world-made-progress.

5. George Ingram and Tony Pipa, "Maximizing U.S.-Korea Development Cooperation in Southeast Asia" (Washington, D.C.: The Brookings Institution, 2019).

6. Chris Humphrey, "Infrastructure Finance in the Developing World: Challenges and Opportunities for Multilateral Development Banks in 21st Century Infrastructure Finance" (Washington, D.C.: The Group of Twenty-Four, June 2015), https://g24.org/wp-content/uploads/2016/05/MARGGK-WP08.pdf.

7. Stromseth, "Don't Make Us Choose."

8. Michele Ruta and others, "Belt and Road Economics: Opportunities and Risks of Transport Corridors" (Washington D.C.: The World Bank, June 18, 2019), www.worldbank.org/en/topic/regional-integration/publication/belt-and-road-economics-opportunities-and-risks-of-transport-corridors.

9. Axel Dreher and others, "Aid, China, and Growth: Evidence from a New Global Development Finance Dataset," Working Paper 46 (Williamsburg, VA: AidData, October 10, 2017), www.aiddata.org/publications/aid-china-and-growth -evidence-from-a-new-global-development-finance-dataset.

10. David Dollar, "Is China's Development Finance a Challenge to the International Order?" *Asian Economic Policy Review* 13, no. 2 (July 2018): 283–298.

11. Wang Mingjie, "China warns US over BRI criticism," *China Daily*, May 10, 2019, http://www.chinadaily.com.cn/a/201905/10/WS5cd54685a3104842260bb06f .html.

12. John Hurley, Scott Morris, and Gailyn Portelance, "Examining the debt implications of the Belt and Road Initiative from a policy perspective" (Washington, D.C.: Center for Global Development, March 2018), www.cgdev.org/publication/ examining-debt-implications-belt-and-road-initiative-a-policy-perspective.

13. "Lao People's Democratic Republic: 2019 Article IV Consultation-Press Release; Staff Report; Statement by the Executive Director for Lao People's Democratic Republic" (Washington, D.C.: International Monetary Fund, Country Report No. 19/267, August 2019), www.imf.org/en/Publications/CR/Issues/2019/08 /08/Lao-Peoples-Democratic-Republic-2019-Article-IV-Consultation -Press-Release-Staff-Report-48577.

14. Keith Zhai and Kay Johnson, "Exclusive: Taking Power—Chinese Firms to Run Laos Electric Grid amid Default Warnings," Reuters, September 15, 2020, https: //www.reuters.com/article/china-laos/exclusive-taking-power-chinese-firm-to-run -laos-electric-grid-amid-default-warnings-idUSL8N2FW068.

15. Ernesto Zedillo, "Repowering the World Bank for the 21st Century: Report of the High Level Commission on Modernization of World Bank Group Governance" (Washington, D.C.: The World Bank Group, October 2009).

16. Alex He, 2016. "China in the International Financial System: A Study of the NDB and the AIIB" (Waterloo, Canada: CIGI Papers, no. 106, June 2016): 3–4, www .cigionline.org/publications/china-international-financial-system-study-ndb-and -aiib.

17. Natalie Lichtenstein, A Comparative Guide to the Asian Infrastructure Investment Bank (Oxford University Press, 2018).

18. Horn, Reinhart, and Trebesch, "Chinese Overseas' Lending."

19. Daniel R. Russel and Blake Berger, "Navigating the Belt and Road Initiative" (Washington, D.C.: Asia Society Policy Institute, June 2019), https://asiasociety.org/ sites/default/files/2019-06/Navigating%20the%20Belt%20and%20Road%20 Initiative_2.pdf.

6

Mobilizing the Indo-Pacific Infrastructure Response to China's Belt and Road Initiative in Southeast Asia

ROLAND RAJAH

INTRODUCTION

The sustainable infrastructure agenda in Southeast Asia has taken on increased prominence in recent years. China's Belt and Road Initiative (BRI) promises a major increase in available funds to help plug the global infrastructure financing gap, including in Southeast Asia. It has also made international infrastructure efforts vastly more contentious. Early enthusiasm from governments participating in the BRI has been replaced with greater caution about the risks. At the same time, there is much geopolitical angst, particularly in the United States, about the role of the BRI as a form of economic statecraft intended to enhance China's influence through state-directed investment and the creation of a more Sino-centric regional order.

This has prompted the United States, as well as Australia and Japan, to respond with their own revamped overseas infrastructure endeavors, including a new Trilateral Partnership for Infrastructure Investment in the Indo-Pacific aimed at coordinating their individual efforts.[1] The primary approach of the trilateral partners is to catalyze more private capital into sustainable infrastructure investment through the use of "blended finance"—using official capital from governments to leverage in private investment.

The key question is: How effective will an approach focused on mobilizing private infrastructure investment be in either competing with the BRI or meeting Southeast Asia's financing needs? This policy brief first describes the infrastructure scene in Southeast Asia and the emerging Indo-Pacific infrastructure strategy of Australia, Japan, and the United States (henceforth, the trilateral partners). It then discusses key infrastructure trends and challenges in Southeast Asia and the prospects of the current trilateral strategy to successfully mobilize significantly more private capital for infrastructure investment. Finally, it puts forward policy ideas for how the trilateral partners might simultaneously promote better development outcomes while responding more effectively to China's growing infrastructure financing role in the region and bolstering their own position.

Though driven by geopolitics, it is vital to recognize that enhanced international policy efforts to channel more capital into infrastructure in Southeast Asia are justified on economic grounds. A large and persistent shortfall in infrastructure investment in the region is a major risk to its future growth prospects and warrants attention—including from external players with an interest in the region's ongoing growth and stability. In addition, the economic case for such investment is made considerably stronger by the presence of persistently low interest rates in most advanced economies. This not only greatly reduces the cost of funding more growth-enhancing infrastructure, but also means that such investment could make an important contribution to providing a much-needed boost to global demand and growth.[2] Seeking to mobilize more private capital also has its merits, as official capital alone could never plug the infrastructure financing gap and there is plenty of (notional) market interest. Finally, the economic pandemic unleashed by COVID-19 only reinforces the importance of the sustainable infrastructure agenda—as a means of supporting the post-crisis recovery and as world interest rates have moved even lower and are likely to remain there for some time.

BRI AND THE EMERGING INDO-PACIFIC
INFRASTRUCTURE RESPONSE

Sustainable infrastructure development is a critical development priority for Southeast Asia. The Asian Development Bank (ADB) has estimated that the region faces an annual financing gap of 3.8–4.1% of GDP or $92–102 billion in constant 2015 prices.[3] Closing the infrastructure financing gap will be essential to not only sustaining Southeast Asia's ongoing economic rise, but also to the need for substantial new investments related to climate change mitigation and adaptation.

China's BRI, first launched in late 2013, ostensibly offers to help meet this financing gap. Southeast Asia is home to flagship BRI investments, including the China-Indochina Peninsula Corridor and the Bangladesh-China-India-Myanmar Economic Corridor, as well as large projects such as the East Coast Railway Link (ECRL) in Malaysia and the Jakarta-Bandung high speed railway project in Indonesia.

However, many high-profile BRI projects have encountered difficulties due to concerns about the impact on sustainability and openness in the region. The fundamental problem afflicting many BRI projects has been a lack of upfront due diligence—in terms of engineering design, economic and financial viability analysis, and environmental and social safeguards—with the result being that many BRI projects have often simply traded speed early in the project cycle for more difficult problems later on.[4] Tied financing (requiring the use of Chinese contractors) and opaque practices have also been associated with cost blow-outs and corruption scandals, most infamously in the case of the ECRL project in Malaysia. These problems have raised concerns, particularly in Washington and other Western capitals, that BRI could contribute to an erosion of fair and open competition, good governance, and economic, environmental, and social sustainability in Southeast Asia (and elsewhere).

In response, Australia, Japan, and the United States have joined together to form a Trilateral Partnership for Infrastructure Investment in the Indo-Pacific. The principle aims are to jointly finance major projects in the region and to coordinate promoting sustainable infrastructure development according to global "high standards"—particularly good governance, open procurement, debt sustainability, and environmental and social safeguards. The new trilateral arrangement is in turn underpinned by actions taken by each partner to enhance their own overseas infrastructure financing capabilities. In particular:

- Australia has revamped its export credit agency, renamed Export Finance Australia, giving it a much wider remit to finance overseas infrastructure projects deemed to be in the broad national interest and substantially increasing its capital base by $1 billion Australian dollars to about AU$1.7 billion, a roughly 150% increase.[5] Australia has also established an AU$2 billion infrastructure financing facility and acquired the ability to effectively provide concessional loans to focus on South Pacific countries, though Timor-Leste will also have access to these developments.[6] Australia also plans to put in place a new aid-funded technical advisory facility to support infrastructure development in the region.[7]

- The United States has transformed its Overseas Private Investment Corporation (OPIC) into a new International Development Finance Corporation (IDFC) with modernized financing capabilities, including the ability to provide equity financing, local currency loans, and guarantees. Also, the United States doubled its total funding portfolio ceiling to $60 billion.[8] The United States has also allocated $113 million to provide technical assistance and advisory support to facilitate greater private infrastructure investment.[9]

- Japan launched its Expanded Partnership for Quality Infrastructure in 2016, which seeks to target over $200 billion in global infrastructure financing over five years to be delivered primarily through the Japan Bank for International Cooperation (JBIC) and the Japan International Cooperation Agency (JICA) as well as "Japan-wide" efforts that incorporate other policy-based financial institutions.[10]

Through these coordinated initiatives, the trilateral Indo-Pacific partners aim to mobilize private capital for regional infrastructure investment, promote sustainable infrastructure development according to global "high standards," and balance China's growing geopolitical influence by providing a competitive alternative. Most recently, the trilateral partners have launched the Blue Dot Network as a multi-stakeholder initiative to evaluate and certify nominated infrastructure projects according to high-quality principles and standards.[11] Further new initiatives may well follow.

INFRASTRUCTURE FINANCING TRENDS AND CHALLENGES IN SOUTHEAST ASIA

The additional resources promised by the trilateral partners are welcome, as is the focus on mobilizing greater private investment. Infrastructure has been growing rapidly as a global asset class, having tripled over the past decade to $420 billion in total assets under management.[12] With the holdings of institutional investors estimated at $100 trillion, there is notionally considerable scope to go much further.[13] This is particularly so, as low global interest rates fuel a search for yield among investors. For investors, infrastructure assets offer the potential for diversification, steady cashflows, and predictable real returns over long time horizons that match well with the needs of institutional investors (for example, pension, insurance and sovereign-wealth funds). For official financiers, involvement from private investors can help to manage different risks and deliver better quality projects.

Supply-side constraints, however, mean that crowding in substantial amounts of additional private capital for infrastructure has been an elusive "holy grail" of development finance for some time. The constraints to greater private investor involvement are well known, including political and macroeconomic risks, corruption, project implementation risks, and problematic legal and regulatory frameworks. These combine with the lower incomes of developing countries to reduce the risk-adjusted returns on offer for investors. The challenge also reflects more technical, though not unrelated, issues, including the lack of well-prepared "bankable" projects, shallow domestic capital markets, and limited country knowledge among potential investors. The World Bank tracks infrastructure projects in developing countries around the world that involve private participation.[14] According to the World Bank, such private participation in infrastructure (PPI) investment has averaged about $110 billion a year over the past decade—providing one-fifth of total investment, or just 13%, of the amount required.[15]

Blended-finance efforts have struggled to crowd in greater private infrastructure investment in the developing world, at least compared to the scale required. For infrastructure projects benefitting from blended finance, the average ratio of private capital "leveraged" per dollar of official finance appears to be in the range of 0.8–1.8.[16] These leverage ratios, however, overestimate the true degree of additionality (that is, that which would not have otherwise occurred) and are in any case well below the degree hoped for given the scale of the infrastructure financing gap.

Overall, the trend in PPI investment across the developing world has been mixed at best—rising during the 2000s but in decline more recently and still below that in the late 1990s (Figure 6-1). This performance is all the more inadequate given ongoing growth in the demand for infrastructure services due to increases in population, urbanization, and economic activity. Further, two-thirds of this investment has flowed to upper-middle-income countries rather than less developed countries where the needs are more acute. The ability to attract private financing has also varied enormously by sector, with power and information and communications technology infrastructure generally more successful, while urban infrastructure—including roads, water, and sanitation—has proven more difficult.[17] In terms of the promise of institutional investor involvement, this has proven largely elusive, with the World Bank finding this provided just 0.7% of private infrastructure investment in the developing world from 2011 to 2017.[18]

FIGURE 6-1. **Limited Progress Lifting Private Participation in Infrastructure Investment**

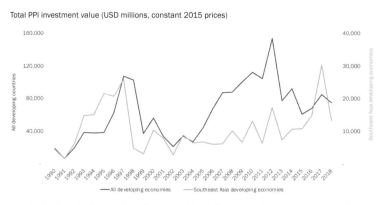

Source: Author's calculations based on World Bank Private Participation in Infrastructure database.

Emerging Southeast Asian economies might seem to offer greater scope for success but in practice appear to largely confront the same constraints as elsewhere. Relative political stability, more dynamic economies, burgeoning pools of urban middle-class consumers, and growing domestic capital markets all mean that Southeast Asia ostensibly offers stronger prospects for leveraging more private capital into infrastructure investment. Yet, overall progress in encouraging greater private infrastructure investment has been disappointing. Total PPI investment amounted to $129 billion over the past decade for developing Southeast Asian economies (that is, excluding Singapore and Brunei).

To put in perspective, such investment was $10.8 billion in 2015, compared to ADB estimates of the current level of infrastructure investment in Association of Southeast Asian Nations (ASEAN) countries of $55 billion in the same year and total required annual investment of $147–$157 billion. That suggests infrastructure investment involving the private-sector accounts for only about one-fifth of actual investment or around 7% of the total needed. From 2011 to 2017, the World Bank can only identify three projects with direct participation from institutional investors with a total investment value of just $2.4 billion from all sources.[19] Nor is the trend in PPI investment any better than elsewhere in the world, having collapsed after the Asian financial crisis, only recently beginning to recover, and still well below the levels of the mid-1990s in real terms (Figure 6-1).

Official finance has played a big role in the recent recovery in private infrastructure investment in Southeast Asia but appears no more successful in mobilizing private capital than elsewhere. Figure 6-2 breaks down the World Bank data to examine the financing sources of PPI investment in Southeast Asia over the past decade. As shown in the left-hand panel, the entire improvement in investment in recent years can be accounted for by projects benefiting from official multilateral and bilateral support—both in terms of direct financing from official agencies as well as "leveraged" private capital.[20] Of note, the majority of official support reflects bilateral, rather than multilateral, financing (Figure 6-2, right-hand panel). Most bilateral financing support has come from just two sources: Japan and China. The ratio of private capital leveraged per dollar of official finance over the past decade in Southeast Asia has been 1.5—suggesting no better success in mobilizing private capital than in other parts of the developing world.[21]

FIGURE 6-2. The Recent Improvement in Private Infrastructure
Investment in Southeast Asia Reflects Increased
Blended Financing (USD Millions, 2009–2018)

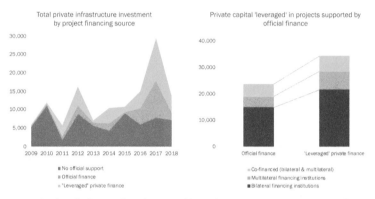

Source: Author's calculations based on World Bank Private Participation in Infrastructure database.

Moreover, the true additionality of this leverage is less than it seems, with signs that private capital is being crowded out. A limited pool of bankable projects means increased official financing may be crowding out private investment that might otherwise have financed the same projects. There are signs this is occurring. For instance, it is notable that the level of PPI investment not receiving official financing support has been flat over the past decade and has only marginally increased since the early 2000s. This is despite progress by Southeast Asian economies in improving their macro-financial stability, strengthening policy and institutional frameworks, and maintaining fast economic growth—though crowding out by domestic state sectors is also a key factor.

Another sign of bilateral financing crowding out private investment can be seen by examining infrastructure projects supported by the multilateral development banks. These tend to be projects where the multilaterals are heavily involved in project preparation and structuring transactions. Projects supported only by the multilaterals have realized an average leverage ratio of 1.7 dollars in private capital per official dollar over the past decade. However, where projects also attract bilateral financing support, this has tended to result in a much lower overall leverage ratio of 1.2.[22] It is possible that these projects were less financially viable than others and therefore in need of greater official sector support. However, compared to the overall portfolio of projects supported by the multilaterals, a disproportionate majority were located in the relatively large and more developed markets of Indonesia and Thailand as opposed to smaller, less developed countries where one would expect the need for official sector support to be greater.

These realities point to the challenge of lifting private infrastructure investment in Southeast Asia given the fundamental supply-side constraints that result in a limited pool of bankable projects. The provision of more technical assistance to assist with reform, project preparation, and transaction advice is one solution that the trilateral partners are pursuing through various new and existing mechanisms. This can surely help.

However, scaling up such efforts is unlikely to unlock significant new pools of bankable infrastructure projects. For instance, recent independent evaluations of the World Bank Group have found that upstream policy reform work failed almost half the time due to political complications and that downstream project structuring and transaction advice had not markedly increased the number of bankable projects.[23] Project preparation facilities appear to have had some success, at least in Asia, and have been expanded, for instance through the establishment of the multi-donor Asia Pacific Project Preparation Facility at the ADB.[24] Nonetheless, these efforts have so far had at most a marginal impact on the overall volume of bankable projects coming through, as can be seen in the disappointing trend in total private infrastructure investment, particularly for that not receiving bilateral financial support.

The difficulty of addressing supply-side constraints poses important challenges and tensions for the agenda of the trilateral partners. If the pool of bankable projects cannot be significantly enlarged, then there is a risk that expanded official financing from the trilateral partners will increasingly suffer from crowding-out effects—resulting in reduced additionality in terms of overall infrastructure investment. It would also go against the stated desire of the trilateral partners to promote open competition following market-based principles. This is especially the case since the trilateral partners have chosen to pursue their enhanced overseas infrastructure efforts primarily through financing mechanisms that largely continue to preference their own firms—that is, "tied financing" not entirely dissimilar to that practiced by China under BRI. This approach not only undermines the claim of the trilateral partners to be promoting market-based competition but will also likely result in weaker economic and developmental benefits for countries receiving the investment—relative to a truly market-based approach—through higher costs, sub-optimal project selection, and more difficulty in balancing the conflicting interests of project firms and national governments (for example, in terms of financial risk-sharing and infrastructure regulatory settings).

Limited prospects for leveraging significant amounts of additional private capital also has important implications for the ability of the trilateral partners to compete with China's scale. Thus far, the United States and Australia are primarily trying to compete in Southeast Asia by leveraging private capital into their own bilateral efforts, rather than responding with a large increase in their own financing. Only Japan has taken a more ambitious approach in combining leveraging efforts with a scaling-up of its already significant overseas infrastructure financing activities. What are the prospects of meaningfully competing with Chinese scale through the current strategy? Getting a sense of the scale of official infrastructure financing from various players is difficult, especially given the opacity of China's overseas financing activities. Figure 6-3 combines data from multiple sources to shed light on this question.

China has overtaken Japan to become the largest bilateral infrastruc-

FIGURE 6-3. **Competing with the Scale of China's Infrastructure Financing in Southeast Asia**

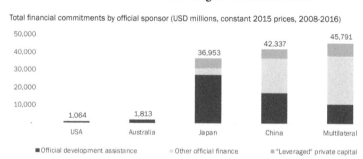

Total financial commitments by official sponsor (USD millions, constant 2015 prices, 2008-2016)

Notes: Figures are compiled based on multiple data sources while removing projects that appear in more than one data source. For China, this is based on ODA-like flows according to AidData. "Leveraged" private capital is based on the World Bank PPI data, which records foreign state-owned enterprises as private firms.

Source: Author's calculations based on World Bank Private Participation in Infrastructure database, OECD Creditor Reporting System, and Custer et al. (2018).

ture financier in Southeast Asia. From 2008 to 2016, China's financial commitments for infrastructure projects totaled $42 billion compared to $37 billion for Japan. The available data only allows us to compile estimates on total official infrastructure financing to 2016. From then on, China's BRI appears to have lost some momentum while Japan's expanded efforts have been gathering pace. Nonetheless, the available data suggests the overall trend has remained intact—with the PPI data extending to the second half of 2019 showing that official infrastructure financing from China continues to outpace that from Japan. Note, this is a very different picture to that suggested by oft-cited estimates compiled by the ratings agency Fitch, which put Japan ahead of China. For our purposes, the Fitch numbers seem questionably large and appear to go well beyond projects receiving official financing support to include projects that might merely involve Japanese and Chinese firms as commercial investors or contractors without any direct financial support from their home governments.[25]

Returning to Figure 6-3, not only has China overtaken Japan in terms of official infrastructure financing, but it has also provided more financing than the trilateral partners combined—owing to the very minor financing roles played by Australia and the United States. Moreover, China is also closing in on the total scale of financing being provided by all multilateral institutions combined. Finally, Figure 6-3 makes clear that leveraged private capital plays only a minor role. Instead, direct financing, including from explicitly concessional sources, plays the dominant role.[26]

The outlook for the future is heavily clouded by the uncertain economic impact of the COVID-19 pandemic, particularly in terms of its differential impact on the economies of the trilateral partners, China, and Southeast Asia. However, on preexisting trends, the ability of the revamped trilateral infrastructure efforts to compete with China's BRI would appear quite uncertain. Recent enhancements to the overseas infrastructure capabilities of Australia and the United States should see some expansion in their financing activities in the region. Yet, any setback to BRI's continued expansion could prove temporary. China as looks to respond to recent criticisms and lift its standards. That could mean a slower pace of expansion for BRI going forward, especially if it involves greater project due diligence and selectivity. Nonetheless, China will likely continue to eschew the kind of risk-averse and time-consuming standards employed by both the trilateral partners and multilateral institutions. To the extent China continues

to be perceived to offer faster, less risk-averse, and more responsive infrastructure support, it is likely to continue to find plenty of willing takers
in Southeast Asia—where most governments are fiscally constrained, are
struggling to attract sufficient private capital inflows, are relatively comfortable with state-led investment, and are keen to further integrate their
economies with China's and capture relocating industrial supply chains.[27]

POLICY RECOMMENDATIONS FOR THE TRILATERAL PARTNERS

**1. The trilateral partners should take active steps to minimize crowding out
and the risk of an overly mercantilist approach.**

Thus far, the trilateral partners have put much more emphasis on financing new infrastructure projects than on increasing the pipeline of
bankable projects. Despite the limitations noted earlier about what results
can realistically be expected, at minimum there should be a commensurate increase in efforts to expand the pool of bankable projects to minimize crowding-out effects and align with the trilateral partners' emphasis
on market-based, rather than state-backed, competition. Similarly, the trilateral partners should articulate clear policies prioritizing the sustainable
development of Southeast Asian economies over any mercantilist interests. That should involve a strong commitment to untied financing and
ensuring projects are structured to prioritize the development interests of
partner countries rather than home-country firms.

**2. The trilateral partners should increase technical assistance, including via
the multilateral development banks, to help Southeast Asian governments
consider and manage BRI projects.**

Governments in the region are well aware of the risks involved with
the BRI. But a lack of technical capacity is often a constraint in mitigating
these risks and putting in place more favorable arrangements. Tactfully
deployed technical assistance could help Southeast Asian governments lift
the standard of any BRI projects they take on. To some extent, this can
be done through carefully managed bilateral facilities operating under
the public radar. A more politically neutral (and therefore more scal-
able) approach would be to work through the multilateral development
banks—including the ADB, World Bank, and even the China-led Asian Infrastructure Investment Bank (of which Australia is a member, though not

Japan or the United States). These institutions already house infrastructure advisory facilities receiving China's financial support and recently signed a joint Memorandum of Understanding with China's finance ministry to establish a cooperation platform. By contrast, the recently announced Blue Dot Network is unlikely to have much impact on raising the standard of BRI projects, as these will likely remain outside the network as long as it is perceived as a U.S.-led effort to counter the BRI.

3. The trilateral partners should not only focus on high infrastructure standards, but also strengthen existing approaches to be more streamlined, less risk-averse, and fit-for-purpose—including via the Blue Dot Network.

The current focus of the trilateral partners on "high standards" risks proving ineffective in competing with China's BRI while paying too little attention to important shortcomings in existing international standards and approaches. While the emphasis on "high standards" is intended to lead to better quality and more sustainable projects, developing country governments, including in Southeast Asia, have tended to see this as resulting in slow and burdensome processes and excessive risk aversion—particularly with regard to the multilateral development banks and in more difficult and fragile environments. Persistent efforts to streamline processes and strike a better balance between managing risks and delivering results are needed. This could provide a useful agenda for the Blue Dot Network in developing common approaches to learning from the experience of national, bilateral, multilateral, and private financing institutions, as well as civil society. This would involve shifting the network toward emphasising fit-for-purpose approaches in addition to promoting "high standards."

4. The trilateral partners should scale up official financing, including aid, to both support greater regional prosperity and keep pace with China as an infrastructure financier for the region.

Contrary to frequent assertions that the West cannot compete with China's financing scale, the figures compiled in this brief show that the trilateral partners already provide almost as much infrastructure financing as China. Moreover, the majority of this comes from aid budgets rather than non-aid sources. Currently, each of the trilateral partners allocates around 0.2% of Gross National Income to official development assistance, well

below around the 0.5% among many European governments.[28] Moving to
the OECD average of 0.3% would be enough to allow the trilateral partners
to compete with China as an infrastructure financier at its current scale
(or avoid being left behind if China increases its financing further). Importantly, this would allow the trilateral partners to compete with China
in infrastructure in Southeast Asia without sacrificing other development
priorities—such as in health, education, and developing other parts of the
world—which remain no less important than before.

Political appetite among the trilateral partners for increasing overseas development spending in the immediate aftermath of the COVID-19
pandemic may however be limited. The political priority will likely be on
meeting domestic spending needs while the politics of increased public
debt may serve as a major constraint (even if government borrowing costs
are expected to remain extremely low for some time). A realistic ambition
might thus be about preserving current spending levels or perhaps achieving only modest increases. Linking increased development financing to
the new geostrategic paradigm and a coordinated approach among the
partners could assist in securing domestic support for this agenda. Additional scale could also be achieved if increased funding were at least partly
channeled toward introducing more concessionality into current blended-
financing efforts. This would help make more potential projects financially
viable—especially critical for less developed countries and poorer areas
within countries where the investment needs are greatest, but financial
viability are most limited.

**5. Australia should consider further steps to enhance its own development
financing capabilities to match those of Japan and the United States.**

Australia is the only trilateral partner that lacks a dedicated international development agency, after integrating its bilateral aid agency into
the Department of Foreign Affairs and Trade six years ago. Australia is
also the only trilateral partner without an ability to directly provide
concessional loans (outside of the Pacific) or more innovative blended-
financing instruments such as development guarantees and equity investments. While Export Finance Australia can deploy a variety of financing
instruments, its focus is on commercial financing and maximizing the
benefits to Australia. rather than concessional financing and sustainable
development. The simplest approach would be to build on the new Pacific

infrastructure financing facility to allow for concessional loans in other regions and a wider range of development financing instruments.[29] A more ambitious option would be to establish a dedicated Australian development finance institution, as the United States, Japan, and other developed country governments have done.

Notes

1. "Joint Statement of the Governments of Australia, Japan, and the United States of America on the Trilateral Partnership for infrastructure investment in the Indo-Pacific," Prime Minister of Australia, November 17, 2018, https://www.pm.gov .au/media/joint-statement-governments-australia-japan-and-united-states.

2. Gauti B. Eggertsson, Neil R. Mehrota, and Lawrence H. Summers, "Secular Stagnation in the Open Economy," *American Economic Review* 106, no. 5 (May 2016): 503–507, https://www.aeaweb.org/articles?id=10.1257/aer.p20161106.

3. "Meeting Asia's Infrastructure Needs" (Manila: Asian Development Bank, 2017), https://www.adb.org/sites/default/files/publication/227496/special-report-in frastructure.pdf.

4. Daniel R. Russel and Blake Berge, "Navigating the Belt and Road Initiative" (New York: The Asia Society Policy Institute, June 2019), https://asiasociety.org/pol icy-institute/belt-and-road-initiative.

5. "Export Finance and Insurance Corporation Amendment (Support for Infrastructure Financing) Bill 2019," Parliament of Australia, https://www.aph.gov .au/Parliamentary_Business/Bills_Legislation/Bills_Search_Results/Result?bId =r6263.

6. The facility will provide AU$1.5 billion in non-concessional loans and AU$0.5 billion in grants. In reality, planned loan terms imply the so-called non-concessional loans will be concessional by OECD standards (though the Australian government has indicated these will not be reported to the OECD as official development assistance). In addition, some projects will involve a blending of loan and grant financing, which will effectively imply the provision of an even more concessional loan. "Australian Infrastructure Financing Facility for the Pacific," Department of Foreign Affairs and Trade, https://www.aiffp.gov.au/.

7. "Investment Design Document for the Southeast Asia Economic Governance and Infrastructure Facility," Department of Foreign Affairs and Trade, December 23, 2019, https://dfat.gov.au/about-us/business-opportunities/Pages/investment -design-document-for-the-southeast-asia-economic-governance-and-infrastruc ture-facility.aspx.

8. "Better Utilization of Investments Leading to Development Act of 2018 or the BUILD Act of 2018," United States Congress, https://www.congress.gov/bill/115th -congress/senate-bill/2463.

9. Michael R. Pompeo, "America's Indo-Pacific Economic Vision" (speech, Washington, DC, July 30, 2018), https://www.state.gov/remarks-on-americas-indo -pacific-economic-vision/.

10. "The 'Expanded Partnership for Quality Infrastructure' initiative directed toward the G7 Ise-Shima Summit Meeting announced," Ministry of Economy, Trade and Industry, May 23, 2016, https://www.meti.go.jp/english/press/2016/0523_01.html.

11. "The Launch of Multi-Stakeholder Blue Dot Network," U.S. International Development Finance Corporation, November 4, 2019, https://www.dfc.gov/media/opic-press-releases/launch-multi-stakeholder-blue-dot-network.

12. "2018 Preqin Global Infrastructure Report" (New York: Preqin, 2018), https://docs.preqin.com/reports/2018-Preqin-Global-Infrastructure-Report-Sample-Pages.pdf.

13. Rabah Arezki, et al., "From Global Savings Glut to Financing Infrastructure: The Advent of Investment Platforms," IMF Working Paper (Washington, DC: International Monetary Fund, February 2016), https://www.imf.org/external/pubs/ft/wp/2016/wp1618.pdf.

14. The World Bank website details what types of projects are included in the database. Of note for purposes here is that foreign state-owned enterprises are included as private actors when operating outside their home country. See "Private Participation in Infrastructure database" (Washington, DC: World Bank), https://ppi.worldbank.org/en/ppi.

15. Fernanda Ruiz-Nuñez and Zichao Wei, "Infrastructure Investment Demands in Emerging Markets and Developing Economies," World Bank Policy Research Working Paper 7414 (Washington DC: World Bank, September 2015), http://documents.worldbank.org/curated/en/141021468190774181/pdf/WPS7414.pdf.

16. Samantha Attridge and Lars Engen, "Blended finance in the poorest countries: the need for a better approach" (London: Overseas Development Institute, April 2019), https://www.odi.org/publications/11303-blended-finance-poorest-countries-need-better-approach; Charles Kenny, "Marginal, Not Transformational: Development Finance Institutions and the Sustainable Development Goals" (Washington, DC: Center for Global Development, September 2019), https://www.cgdev.org/sites/default/files/PP156-Kenny-Marginal-Not-Transformational.pdf.

17. Judith E. Tyson, "Private infrastructure financing in developing countries" (London: Overseas Development Institute, August 2018), https://www.odi.org/sites/odi.org.uk/files/resource-documents/12366.pdf.

18. "Contribution of Institutional Investors Private Investment in Infrastructure 2011–H1 2017" (Washington, DC: World Bank, 2018), https://ppi.worldbank.org/content/dam/PPI/documents/PPI_InstitutionalInvestors_Update_2017.pdf.

19. Ibid.

20. Leveraged private capital is calculated as total investment minus identified official financing support from multilateral, bilateral, and domestic government sources. Given the definition of PPI used by the World Bank, this does not strictly exclude non-private sources of finance. However, the data indicates the majority of investment has been private (noting that the PPI data treats foreign state-owned enterprises as private).

21. Kenny, "Marginal, Not Transformational." Kenny estimates a global leverage ratio of 1.8 using PPI data.

22. For cofinanced projects, the leverage ratio is the ratio between total official financing (both bilateral and multilateral) and private financing.

23. "World Bank Group Support to Public-Private Partnerships" (Washington, DC: Independent Evaluation Group, 2013), https://ieg.worldbankgroup.org/eval uations/world-bank-group-support-ppp; "The International Finance Corporation's Approach to Engaging Clients for Increased Development Impact" (Washington, DC: Independent Evaluation Group, 2017), https://ieg.worldbankgroup.org/ evaluations/ifc-client-engagement.

24. David Bray, et al., "Assessment of the Effectiveness of Project Preparation Facilities in Asia" (Toronto: G20 Development Working Group, September 2014), http://g20.org.tr/wp-content/uploads/2014/12/assessment-effectiveness-ppfs-in -asia-15092014.pdf.

25. Fitch Solutions has compiled alternative figures to those presented in this policy brief that suggest that Japanese infrastructure financing in Southeast Asia is larger than that from China, with $367 billion in Japanese infrastructure projects in Southeast Asia under preparation or construction, compared to $255 billion for China. However, the basis of these figures is unclear and, given the scale estimated, would appear to go well beyond projects supported by official finance. It may, for instance, include purely commercial investments involving no official financing as well as projects where Japanese or Chinese firms are involved only as construction or engineering contractors. Even then, the figures seem large, considering ADB estimates that total annual infrastructure investment in Southeast Asia from all sources was only $55 billion in 2015. "China No Match for Japan in Southeast Asia Infrastructure Race," Bloomberg, June 23, 2019, https://www.bloomberg.com/news/articles/2019-06 -23/china-no-match-for-japan-in-southeast-asia-infrastructure-race.

26. Official development assistance is by definition concessional in nature. However, other official finance is also often provided on terms considerably better than that available from the market.

27. For instance, see comments by Malaysian Prime Minister Mahathir Mohamad, despite the issues experienced with the ECRL project: Marian Zhou, "Mahathir: 'We have to go to the Chinese' for infrastructure," Nikkei Asian Review, September 27, 2019, https://asia.nikkei.com/Politics/International-relations/ Mahathir-We-have-to-go-to-the-Chinese-for-infrastructure2.

28. "Net ODA," Organisation for Economic Cooperation and Development, https://data.oecd.org/oda/net-oda.htm.

29. An independent study was commissioned to recommend potential options, but the status of the report has remained unclear for over a year. See Stephen Howes, "Possible downsides to a new international development policy," DevPolicy Blog, February 4, 2020, https://devpolicy.org/possible-downsides-to-new-international -development-policy-20200204/.

7

ASEAN Economic Prospects amid Emerging Turbulence

Development Challenges and Implications for Reform

KHUONG VU

INTRODUCTION

The Association of Southeast Asian Nations (ASEAN) comprises ten countries: Brunei, Cambodia, Indonesia, Laos, Malaysia, Myanmar, the Philippines, Singapore, Thailand, and Vietnam (Table 7-1). Situated between two rising economic powers, China and India, ASEAN countries are facing enormous direct opportunities and challenges brought about by the rise of these two giants in a rapidly changing global environment.

Encompassing more than 650 million people, the ASEAN economy is relatively large, comparable to India in terms of gross domestic product (GDP) (Table 7-1). The ten ASEAN countries, however, vary greatly by income and development level, from Myanmar and Cambodia, which are among the poorest countries, to Singapore and Brunei, which are among the wealthiest nations.

To better project the future prospects of ASEAN countries, it is important to comprehend the three prevailing distinctive features of the region: harmonious diversity, development aspirations, and an embrace of global integration. In terms of harmonious diversity, the ten countries have different religions, population sizes, political systems, and levels of economic development. However, their substantial, sustained efforts to promote peace, partnership, and integration have been impressive. The formation of the ASEAN Economic Community (AEC) in 2015 marked a major milestone in such efforts. In terms of development aspirations, ASEAN has surprised the world with not only with the success of Singapore, but also the new waves of reforms in member states, ranging from Vietnam and Myanmar to Indonesia and the Philippines. In terms of embracing global integration, ASEAN as an economic bloc is one of the top worldwide destinations for foreign direct investment (FDI), and its trade-to-GDP ratio exceeds 100% (Table 7-1).

TABLE 7-1. **ASEAN in a Snapshot, 2018**

Country	Population		Current GDP (billion)		Current GDP per capita		Global integration*					
	Millions of people	2008-2018 growth	US $	PPP $	US $	PPP $	Trade-to-GDP ratio	Exports	Imports	Total trade	Trade balance	FDI inflows
Brunei	0.4	1.2%	13.6	34.7	31,628	80,778	93%	7	5.7	12.7	1.4	0.5
Cambodia	16.2	1.6%	24.6	70.8	1,512	4,354	163%	18.4	21.8	40.2	-3.4	3.1
Indonesia	267	1.3%	1,040	3,490	3,894	13,057	41%	208.7	216.2	425	-7.5	20
Laos	7.1	1.6%	18.1	52.6	2,568	7,441	75%	6.2	7.3	13.5	-1.1	1.3
Malaysia	31.5	1.4%	354	999	11,239	31,698	132%	246.5	221.3	467.8	25.1	8.6
Myanmar	53.7	0.7%	71.2	358	1,326	6,662	49%	15.8	18.9	34.6	-3.1	1.3
Philippines	107	1.6%	331	953	3,103	8,935	65%	89.1	127.7	216.8	-38.5	9.8
Singapore	5.6	1.5%	364	571	64,582	101,353	326%	642.3	545.5	1,187.8	96.7	82
Thailand	69.4	0.4%	505	1,320	7,274	19,018	123%	336.3	285.1	621.4	51.2	13.3
Vietnam	95.6	1.0%	245	710	2,564	7,435	206%	258.5	245.6	504.1	12.9	15.5
ASEAN	**653.5**	**1.2%**	**2,966.5**	**8,559**	**4,539**	**13,097**	**119%**	**1,828.8**	**1,695.2**	**3,524.1**	**133.6**	**155.4**
China-India												
China	**1,390**	**0.5%**	**13,600**	**25,400**	**9,771**	**18,210**	**38%**	**2,651**	**2,548.1**	**5,199.1**	**102.9**	**203**
India	**1,350**	**1.2%**	**2,730**	**10,500**	**2,106**	**7,762**	**43%**	**537**	**643**	**1,180**	**-105.9**	**42.1**

Data source: World Development Indicators (WDI). With the exception of trade-to-GDP ratio, measures on "global integration" are in billions of U.S. dollars.

This chapter examines recent developments in ASEAN countries and the impacts of ongoing global turbulence, the U.S.-China trade war, and the COVID-19 crisis on ASEAN economies. The chapter discusses the strategic priorities that ASEAN countries should take in formulating strategies to achieve their development aspirations.

ASEAN'S ECONOMIC CATCH-UP PERFORMANCE, 1998–2018

The Asian financial crisis erupted in 1997, and its severe impact on Asian economies was thought to have put an end to the Asian economic miracles.[1] However, most ASEAN economies have emerged from the crisis stronger and with greater development aspirations.

Using the U.S. income level as the benchmark, one can assess the catch-up performance of a given country during a period by examining how much the country's income has changed over this period relative to the U.S. income. These dynamics can be captured by the catch-up performance index (CUPI), defined as the gap between the country and the United States on per capita growth over the period of study (see Appendix 7-A for detailed construction of this index).

Table 7-2 reports the CUPI and its related information for ASEAN countries during the two decades since the Asian financial crisis (1998–2018). To provide comparative insights, the results for ASEAN's two neighboring giants, China and India, are also reported. Table 7-2 reveals three notable insights.

First, all ASEAN countries, with the exception of Brunei, were among the top 50 performers in the global dynamics of economic catch-up from 1998 to 2018. Brunei's very low performance (ranked 171st out of 179 economies worldwide) can be explained by its already very high per capita income and its oil dominant economy.

Second, the four least-developed ASEAN countries—Myanmar, Cambodia, Laos, and Vietnam—are among the world's top fifteen performers by CUPI. In addition, the convergence trend among ASEAN countries in terms of per capita income from 1998 to 2018 is solid, with its coefficient of variation (CV) sharply declining from 1.5 to 1.1.

Third, if the ASEAN countries are considered one economy, its global rank in the global dynamics of catch-up from 1998 to 2018 is 36th, with a CUPI of 2.4. That is, the ASEAN economy as a whole is well behind that

TABLE 7-2. ASEAN GDP Growth and Catch-up Performance, 1998–2018

(ASEAN countries are in decreasing order by CUPI)

Economy	GDP Growth (%)	Catch-up performance		Relative income per capita (US=100)*	
		CUPI	Global rank	1998	2018
ASEAN	**3.76**	**2.44**	**~36**	**12.8**	**20.9**
Myanmar	9.05	7.73	1	2.4	10.6
Cambodia	6.20	4.87	6	2.7	6.9
Laos	5.49	4.16	10	5.3	11.9
Vietnam	5.30	3.97	13	5.5	11.9
Indonesia	3.67	2.34	38	13.2	20.8
Thailand	3.44	2.11	43	20.1	30.3
Philippines	3.36	2.04	45	9.6	14.3
Singapore	3.35	2.03	46	108.5	161.9
Malaysia	3.28	1.95	50	34.6	50.5
Brunei	-0.59	-1.92	171	188.8	129
China	**8.42**	7.10	2	7.5	29.1
India	**5.22**	3.90	14	5.8	12.4
ASEAN convergence trend					
Mean (M)				38.8	45.4
Standard deviation (SD)				57.7	51.4
Coefficient of variation (CV=SD/M)				1.5	1.1

Source: Author's calculation from the World Bank's WDI database.

*Using per capita GDP measured in current PPP$. The U.S. GDP per capita growth from 1998 to 2018 is 1.32%.

of China (rank=2nd; CUPI=7.1) and India (14th; 3.9) in this catch-up performance. More specifically, ASEAN as a whole trailed India by approximately 1.5 percentage points and China by 4.7 percentage points on the average annual GDP growth rate from 1998 to 2018. These growth gaps suggest that ASEAN countries have the potential to collectively enhance market efficiency and could achieve more robust growth if they were more integrated and better coordinated as one single market.

ASEAN COUNTRIES' DEVELOPMENT ASPIRATIONS

Inspired by the Asian economic miracles, particularly Singapore, and recent development experiences, ASEAN countries have set aspirational development goals in the upcoming decades. As summarized in Table 7-3, while Singapore has become one of the wealthiest nations, the remaining nine nations all exhibit a clear ambition to rapidly build prosperity. More specifically, Brunei aims to be among the world's top ten in both per capita income and quality of life by 2035, while Malaysia, Thailand, Indonesia, the Philippines, Vietnam, Cambodia, Laos, and Myanmar all have set a clear goal of achieving a high development status in the next twenty-five years. If ASEAN countries jointly achieve their visions, the region will be not much behind the European Union in 2050.

ASEAN countries' strong aspiration to close the development gap with advanced countries is motivated by three interrelated factors. First, the strategy for building a prosperous nation is no longer a myth. In particular, the success of a new wave of high-performing Asian economies—including China, India, Vietnam, and Bangladesh—has made the lessons for achieving high economic growth more convincing and straightforward. Among these lessons, adopting a market economy, improving the business environment, embracing globalization to attract foreign direct investment and promote exports, upgrading infrastructure, and investing in human capital development have become canonical tenets in the economic policies of most ASEAN nations (see Appendix 7-D).

Second, globalization has brought enormous benefits to ASEAN countries, ranging from an influx of foreign direct investments and international tourists to the rapid expansion of Asia-based global value chains and the strategic advantage of ASEAN countries as an alternative destination for the "China plus one" strategy adopted by multinational companies.

Third, the information and communications technology (ICT) revolution, with its rapid progress and penetration, has brought unprecedented opportunities for late-comer countries to leapfrog in building their foundations for economic development, especially in communications, connectivity with the developed world, learning, and technology acquisition. As such, the ICT revolution in particular has indeed enabled less-developed countries to reap greater economic development benefits from their "backwardness" advantage.[2] As the digital revolution, including artificial intelligence (AI), is rapidly progressing, researchers foresee trends in both divergence and convergence among countries. The divergence trend is determined principally by sizable disparities in digital infrastructure, digital access, and digital skills. Although these disparities are considerable among ASEAN countries, the region is expected to follow a convergence trend. One of the major drivers of this convergence is the leapfrogging capabilities of the digital technologies and the benchmarking exercises adopted by most ASEAN countries, which foster continuous learning and improvement efforts.

Vietnam can serve as a good example of how a less-developed ASEAN country can embrace the aforementioned factors to make progress in economic development. For example, look at Vietnam's performance vis-à-vis the five G-7 economies that have similar population sizes as Vietnam: France, Germany, Italy, Japan, and the United Kingdom. As shown in Table 7-3, Vietnam caught up with these five G-7 economies in terms of manufacturing employment size during the period 2005 to 2017 (for which data are available). This catch-up performance is even more pronounced for the ICT manufacturing industry.[3] At the same time, although Vietnam remains far below those five economies on labor productivity, its labor productivity growth showed strong catch-up progress in the manufacturing sector and the ICT manufacturing industry. By the same token, although Vietnam was still well below the five nations in merchandise export value and the number of international tourist arrivals in 2018, the country has grown far more rapidly during the past two decades and substantially narrowed the gaps in these two indicators. In terms of embracing the ICT revolution, Vietnam has also shown that it is not too far behind these industrialized nations in terms of the basic indicators capturing ICT penetration (internet and social media usage) and ICT infrastructure quality (mobile internet speed) (Table 7-4). This progress has strengthened Viet-

TABLE 7-3. ASEAN Countries' Development Ambition

Country	Development ambition	Document (year of issue)
Brunei	Joining the world's top 10 in quality of life and per capita income in 2035	Vision 2035 (2004)[2]
Cambodia	Aiming to become an upper-middle-income nation by 2030 and a developed country by 2050	Prime Minister Hun Sen's statement (2013)[3]
Indonesia	Becoming an advanced and prosperous nation among the world's largest five economies by 2045	The Vision of Indonesia 2045 (2019)[4]
Laos	Becoming an upper-middle-income country by 2035	The 8th Five-Year National Socioeconomic Development Plan, 2016-2020 (2016)[5]
Malaysia	Elevating the country's status to a developed economy by 2020	The 11th Malaysia Plan (2015)[6]
Myanmar	People working together to build a brighter future in a pluralistic and prosperous nation	The Myanmar Sustainable Development Plan, 2018-2030 (2018)[7]
Philippines	Becoming a prosperous middle-class society free of poverty by 2040	Our Ambition 2040 (2015)[8]
Singapore	Envisioning a "Smart Nation" that is a leading economy powered by digital innovation, and a world-class city	Singapore's Smart Nation initiative (2014)[9]
Thailand	Turning Thailand into a developed country by 2037	National strategy Thailand 4.0 (2018)[10]
Vietnam	Becoming among the top three ASEAN countries in industry by 2030, with some of its industries being globally competitive; becoming a modern industrialized country by 2045	The Political Bureau Resolution No. 23-NQ/TW (2018)[11]

a. "Brunei is diversifying its energy sources in line with Wawasan Brunei 2035," *The ASEAN Post*, May 2, 2018, https://theaseanpost.com/article/brunei-diversifying-its-energy-sources-line-wawasan-brunei-2035.

b. Phak Seangly, "'Developed' by 2050: PM," *The Phnom Penh Post*, June 7, 2013, https://www.phnompenhpost.com/national/%E2%80%98developed%E2%80%99-2050-pm.

c. Friski Riana, "Jokowi's Vision for Indonesia: World's Largest Economy by 2045," *Tempo*, May 9, 2019, https://en.tempo.co/read/1203633/jokowis-vision-for-indonesia-worlds-largest-economy-by-2045.

d. "8th Five-Year National Socioeconomic Development Plan (2016–2020)," Lao PDR, Ministry of Planning and Investment, June 2016, http://www.la.one.un.org/media-center/publications/258-8th-five-year-national-socio-economic-development-plan-2016-2020.

e. "Malaysia unveils 2020 development vision," *World Bulletin*, May 21, 2015, www.worldbulletin.net/asia-pacific/malaysia-unveils-2020-development-vision-h159498.html.

f. "Myanmar Sustainable Development Plan (2018–2030)," The Republic of the Union of Myanmar, Ministry of Planning and Finance, August 2018, https://themimu.info/sites/themimu.info/files/documents/Core_Doc_Myanmar_Sustainable_Development_Plan_2018_-_2030_Aug2018.pdf.

g. "Vision 2040 Public Consultations: Discussions with the Filipino Youth," Republic of the Philippines, National Economic and Development Authority, 2017, http://www.neda.gov.ph/vision2040/.

h. "Transforming Singapore Through Technology," *Smart Nation*, June 12, 2020, www.smartnation.gov.sg/why-Smart-Nation/transforming-singapore.

i. "Thailand: A Vision For The Future," *Forbes*, October 31, 2018, www.forbes.com/custom/2018/10/30/thailand-a-vision-for-the-future/.

j. "Party sets industrial development goals for 2030," *Vietnam Law Magazine*, May 3, 2018, http://vietnamlawmagazine.vn/party-sets-industrial-development-goals-for-2030-6220.html.

Indicator	Vietnam	France	Germany	Italy	Japan	U.K.
Manufacturing sector[a]						
Employment, in thousands of workers						
2005	3,099	3,662	7,004	3,837	7,549	3,138
2017	7,651	2,818	7,189	3,211	7,820	2,522
CAGR (2005-2017)	7.8%	-2.2%	0.2%	-1.5%	0.3%	-1.8%
Labor productivity (value-added per worker), U.S. dollars						
2005	3,236	72,678	76,253	67,841	124,397	83,496
2017	8,902	91,239	88,723	80,408	116,969	89,195
CAGR (2005-2017)	8.8%	1.9%	1.3%	1.4%	-0.5%	0.6%
ICT manufacturing industry (ISIC=30)a						
Employment, in thousands of workers						
2005	11	9	42	12	118	28
2017	693	129	348	82	1,262	111
CAGR (2005-2017)	41.0%	24.9%	19.4%	17.3%	21.8%	12.1%
Labor productivity (value-added per worker)						
2005	10,824	69,984	113,035	59,138	128,546	84,183
2017	21,013	104,599	102,272	79,357	121,036	104,496
CAGR (2005-2017)	5.7%	3.4%	-0.8%	2.5%	-0.5%	1.8%
Merchandise exports (U.S. billions of dollars)[b]						
1998	9.4	320.6	543.8	245.8	387.9	273.9
2018	15.5	89.3	38.9	61.6	31.2	36.3
CAGR (1998-2018)	17.7%	3.0%	5.4%	4.1%	3.3%	2.9%
International tourist arrivals (millions)[b]						
1998	1.5	70.1	16.5	34.9	4.1	23.7
2018	15.5	89.3	38.9	61.6	31.2	36.3
CAGR (1998-2018)	12.3%	1.2%	4.4%	2.9%	10.7%	2.2%
ICT penetration (per 100 people)[c]						
Internet users	70.4	92.3	96.0	92.5	93.8	94.9
Facebook users	68.5	50.4	37.6	50.7	22.1	65.7
ICT infrastructure (March 2020)[d]						
Mobile internet speed (Mbps)	33.97	43.04	37.31	30.30	35.73	35.39

Sources: [a] UNIDO industrial database; [b] WDI database; [c] Internet World Stat; [d] Global Speeds
March 2020.

nam's confidence and capability in adopting a more vigorous economic catch-up strategy in the coming years. It should be noted that this confidence would have been considered a mere fantasy only a decade ago. At the same time, the country's development journey will be long and challenging because its current labor productivity is only one-tenth that of any G-7 economy, while the economic development landscape in the years ahead has become much less favorable and predictable than in the past three decades.

EMERGING TURBULENCES AND ASEAN VULNERABILITIES

As the development landscape has changed in favor of economic transformation and growth in ASEAN countries, two major global turbulences have emerged. The first is the U.S.-China trade war, which began in 2018. The trade tension has slowed down the world's GDP growth from a 3.5% average in 2016–2018 to 2.9% in 2019, and adversely affected many economies.[4] The second is the COVID-19 pandemic, which erupted in Wuhan, China in late 2019. The impacts of this crisis are unthinkably extensive and severe, and the world economy is projected to fall in deep recession in 2020.

To make a rough assessment of the vulnerability of a given economy to each of these shocks, one can create a simple index, which is calculated as the gap in GDP growth between the rate observed for the "damage" year and the rate averaged for the three previous years.[5] For the U.S.-China trade war, the "damage" year is 2019, and its previous three-year period is 2016–2018; for the COVID-19 pandemic, the "damage" year is 2020, and its previous three-year period is 2017–2019. As the U.S.-China trade war and the COVID-19 crisis are two consecutive events, the index of their combined effect, which is calculated as a simple sum of the two effects, can reveal further insights. The sign and magnitude of the index for a country with regard to a given shock indicates the degree of the country's vulnerability to the shock.

Table 7-5 reports these indexes for countries in three Asian regions: ASEAN, South Asia (Bangladesh, Bhutan, India, Nepal, Pakistan, and Sri Lanka) and Northeast Asia (China, Hong Kong, Mongolia, South Korea, and Taiwan). Table 7-5 reveals three notable findings.

First, the impact of the U.S.-China trade war on ASEAN countries in

The economies in each group are in decreasing order by the combined effect of the U.S.-China trade war and COVID-19.)

Economy/ region	Annual GDP growth				Vulnerability**		
	2016-2018 average	2019	2017-2019 average	2020*	U.S.-China trade war	COVID-19 crisis*	Combined effect
	(A)	(B)	(C)	(D)	(I)	(II)	(III)
World	3.6	2.9	3.5	-3	-0.7	-6.5	-7.2
ASEAN (Median)					-0.4	-5.5	-6.7
Thailand	3.8	2.4	3.5	-6.7	-1.4	-10.2	-11.7
Cambodia	7.2	7.1	7.2	-1.6	-0.1	-8.8	-8.9
Singapore	3.3	0.7	2.5	-3.5	-2.6	-6.0	-8.6
Malaysia	5.0	4.3	4.9	-1.7	-0.7	-6.6	-7.3
Laos	6.7	5	6.1	0.7	-1.7	-5.4	-7.1
Philippines	6.6	5.9	6.3	0.6	-0.7	-5.7	-6.4
Indonesia	5.1	5	5.1	0.5	-0.1	-4.6	-4.7
Myanmar	6.3	6.8	6.6	1.8	0.5	-4.8	-4.3
Vietnam	6.7	7	7.0	2.7	0.3	-4.3	-4.0
Brunei	-0.4	3.9	1.8	1.3	4.3	-0.5	3.8
South Asia (Median)					-1.0	-4.6	-4.8
Pakistan	5.6	3.3	4.9	-1.5	-2.3	-6.4	-8.7
India	7.4	5	6.3	1.9	-2.4	-4.4	-6.8
Bangladesh	7.4	8.2	7.8	2	0.8	-5.8	-5.0
Sri Lanka	3.7	2.6	3.1	-0.5	-1.1	-3.6	-4.7
Nepal	5.2	7.1	7.3	2.5	1.9	-4.8	-2.9
Bhutan	5.3	4.4	4.0	2.7	-0.9	-1.3	-2.2
Northeast Asia (Median)					-0.6	-6.4	-6.3
Hong Kong	3.0	-1.2	1.6	-4.8	-4.1	-6.4	-10.5
Taiwan	2.7	2.7	2.9	-4	0.0	-6.9	-6.9
Mongolia	4.6	5.1	5.9	-1	0.5	-6.9	-6.3
China	6.7	6.1	6.5	1.2	-0.6	-5.3	-5.9
South Korea	2.9	2	2.6	-1.2	-0.9	-3.8	-4.8

Note: Numbers may not add up due to rounding. The combined effect for a group is the median value of the combined effects calculated for its members.

Sources: Data on actual GDP growth for 2016 to 2019 are from ADB (2020), https://data.adb.org/dataset/gdp-growth-asia-and-pacific-asiandevelopment-outlook; GDP growth forecasts for 2020 and 2021 are from the International Monetary Fund (IMF, 2020), https://www.imf.org/external/datamapper/NGDP_RPCH@WEO/OEMDC/ADVEC/WEOWORLD. The GDP growth forecasts for 2020 from the IMF (2020) may be further adjusted as real-world situations unfold. For a given country and the world, the three vulnerability indexes are calculated as follows: (I)=(B)-(A); (II)=(D)-(C); (III)=(I)+(II).

2019 was mixed. While the index is negative and large for Singapore, Laos, and Thailand, which implies a severe loss, it is positive for Vietnam, Myanmar, and Brunei, which suggests some notable gains for these countries. At the group level (based on the index's median value), the vulnerability of ASEAN countries is much lower than that of the other two Asian groups, as well as of the whole world. The mixed effect of the U.S.-China trade war can be explained as follows. While the trade tension has caused a slowdown in global demand, it has increased FDI inflows in ASEAN countries, as multinational companies have increasingly decided to shift some of their activity out of China (see Appendix 7-C for some illustrative evidence).

Second, ASEAN countries are being severely affected by the COVID-19 crisis. With the exception of Brunei, the vulnerability is substantial for all countries in the bloc, ranging from –4.3 for Vietnam to –10.2 for Thailand. In particular, forecasted GDP growth for 2020 is negative for four countries (Thailand, Singapore, Malaysia, and Cambodia) and plunges by more than four to five percentage points for five others (Vietnam, Laos, Myanmar, the Philippines, and Indonesia). At the group level (based on the index's median value), the vulnerability of ASEAN countries is also more severe than in South Asia, but less severe than in Northeast Asia and the whole world.

Third, ASEAN countries as a group are far more vulnerable than both South Asia and Northeast Asia in the vulnerability index for the combined effect. This finding implies that the development road ahead for ASEAN economies will be even rockier if new turbulences emerge.

ASEAN DEVELOPMENT PROSPECTS AND
STRATEGIC PRIORITIES FOR REFORM

While the degree of economic damage caused by the U.S.-China trade war and the COVID-19 crisis may vary by country and region, these two consecutive shocks convey the same message to all: The world has reached an inflection point that requires fundamental changes. This message is particularly relevant for ASEAN countries, the growth model for which has been largely built on the favorable conditions brought about by the transformative power of three forces: globalization, the ICT revolution, and the rise of Asia. In this rapidly changing environment, ASEAN countries, with the exception of Singapore, have mainly relied on a basic framework for prosperity creation that emphasizes five priorities: macroeconomic stability, business environment improvement, global integration, infrastructure upgrading, and human capital development.

While the aforementioned basic framework for prosperity creation remains valid and essential, the new development landscape requires three strategic shifts in the development strategy of each country:

- The first is to shift the management focus from reacting to events to proactively building a foundation that ensures that the economy will be prepared, competitive, and resilient in a VUCA (volatile, uncertain, complex, and ambiguous) environment.[6] In this strategic shift, digital transformation, government effectiveness, transparency, productivity, innovation, and trust-building should be top priorities for reform efforts. For productivity growth, shifting resources from low- to high-value activity, with vigorous efforts in restructuring and technology acquisition, should have a higher priority than promoting investment for simple production expansion. As the lessons of Asian economic miracle have shown, this foresighted approach plays a crucial role in the economic catch-up success of a poor nation.[7]

- The second is to shift the development focus from mobilizing resources in order to seize opportunities to building up strategic capabilities to cope with unexpected challenges and create long-term value. In this shift, exploiting the country's existing advantages must come with strenuous efforts to build its strategic strengths, diligently addressing its inherent and emergent vulnerabilities. For example, Vietnam has enthusiastically embraced the "Quad-Plus" initiative, as apparent in the prime minister's decision to form a special task force to attract new waves of FDI to Vietnam. This proactive strategy, however, is effective only if the country makes unprecedented efforts to overcome its inherent weaknesses, especially lack of transparency, rampant corruption, and low effectiveness in promoting technology acquisition and innovation.

- The third is to shift the prosperity-building focus from the narrow scope of each individual country to the broad interest of the entire ASEAN community, which would upgrade the status and competitiveness of all member states. In this shift, fostering regional integration, synergistic effects, and coordination capabilities can bring considerable gains to every member nation. It should be noted that ASEAN leaders adopted the AEC in November 2015 as a blueprint to transform ASEAN into a single economy. While the formation of AEC has laid a foundation for building momentum toward ASEAN synergy, it still has a long way to go.

Powerful momentum could emerge if ASEAN countries can work together to promote the "ASEAN consensus" development model presented in Appendix 7-D. This model, which offers a meaningful alternative to the two existing competing development models—the "Washington consensus" and "Beijing Consensus"—emphasizes the three major pillars of an effective economic development strategy in the twenty-first century: synergy, vigor, and sustainability.

CONCLUSION

The U.S.-China trade war and the COVID-19 crisis are not only global shocks with immediate and substantial consequences, but also a signal that the development landscape will face heightened uncertainty and formidable challenges in the time ahead. As all ASEAN countries have established aspirational goals to achieve considerable economic progress in the next few decades, they should turn these emerging threats into a unique opportunity to raise the sense of urgency for change and deepen their commitment to fundamental and visionary reform efforts. ASEAN countries should also focus on formulating an effective strategy to build synergy among themselves and with the world. Positioning themselves as a group of countries that care not only about their own fitness but also the fitness of others (that of region and the whole world) in the post-COVID-19 economic evolution will make ASEAN much stronger and more cohesive.

ASEAN is one of the main theaters for U.S.-China tensions. As these tensions have been further intensified amid the COVID-19 pandemic,[8] the region has an important role to play in shaping the direction of this crucial geopolitical relationship. ASEAN should not only avoid taking sides, but also adopt a proactive approach to make the relationship less unproductive, if not outright productive. A core principle for ASEAN action in this endeavor is to encourage both the United States and China not to prove who exhibits greater strength; rather, they key question is about who is the better fit for a new era of development and more capable of enhancing the fitness of ASEAN countries during the coming phase of global economic evolution.

APPENDIX 7-A. Construction of the Catch-up Performance Index (CUPI)

The catch-up performance index (CUPI) is defined as follows:[19]

$$CUPI_{0,T}^i = ln\left[\frac{rel\_y_T^i}{rel\_y_0^i}\right]/T * 100 \quad (1)$$

where $CUPI_{0,T}^i$ is the CUPI of country i over period [0, T] and $rel\_y_t^i$ is relative per capita income measured in purchasing power parity (PPP) dollars at constant prices of country in year in comparison to the U.S. ($rel\_y_t^i = y_t^i/y_t^{US}$).

By definition, if country i is catching up or forging ahead, its relative income improves, $rel\_y_T^i > rel\_y_0^i$, which means $CUPI_{0,T}^i$ >0. Conversely, if country is falling behind, its relative income gap with the U.S. deteriorates, $rel\_y_T^i > rel\_y_0^i$, which means $CUPI_{0,T}^i$ <0.

That is, the sign and magnitude of the CUPI index provide a meaningful measure to assess the catch-up performance of a given country in terms of per capita income over the period under investigation.

*For more details, see Khuong Vu, "Sources of Growth in the World Economy: A Comparison of G7 and E7 Economies," in *Measuring Economic Growth and Productivity: Foundations, KLEMS Production Models, and Extensions*, ed. Barbara Fraumeni (Cambridge, MA: Academic Press, 2019).

APPENDIX 7-B. Determinants of Economic Growth

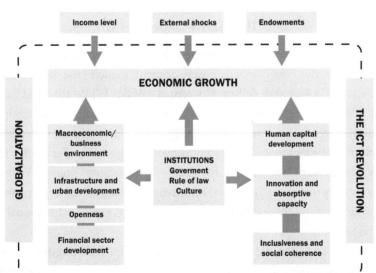

APPENDIX 7-C. **Net FDI Inflows from the United States
to Asian Countries, 2019 versus 2018**

(Countries are in increasing order of the change in FDI inflows from 2018 to 2019.)

Country	2018 (A)	2019 (B)	Change (B)-(A)
China	7,592	5,113	-2,479
Malaysia	-88	-2,157	-2,069
Taiwan	529	-47	-576
Philippines	689	302	-387
Hong Kong	1,242	944	-298
Thailand	44	1,126	1,082
South Korea	-455	1,564	2,019
India	2,080	4,952	2,872
Japan	3,289	6,609	3,320
Indonesia	-3,051	1,351	4,402
Singapore	-47,508	24,478	71,986
Others (Vietnam, Cambodia, etc.)	835	942	107

Source: The U.S. Bureau of Economic Analysis (BEA) database, https://www.bea.gov/data/intl-trade-investment/direct-investment-country-and-industry.

APPENDIX 7-D. **The ASEAN Consensus (ADC) Model**

Policymakers in developing countries have, to some extent, been influenced by the two competing development models: the Washington consensus (WAC) and Beijing Consensus (BEC). While the WAC and BEC—which were introduced by John Williamson and Joshua Cooper Ramos, respectively—offer valuable insights for policy reforms to promote economic development, they are not robust enough to be effective for the new development landscape in the twenty-first century.[9] Khuong Vu and Kris Hartley introduce the ASEAN Consensus (ADC) model, arguing for a strategic focus on three core components: synergy, vigor, and sustainability (Figure D1).[10]

Compared to the WAC and BEC, the ADC model distinguishes itself in three particular ways (Table D1): first, its primary focus is on the "why" question, while the other two models concern "what" and "how" questions; second, the ADC focuses on value creation as articulated by a comprehensive framework that includes synergy, vigor, and sustainability (by contrast, the WAC is preoccupied with market efficiency and the BEC with coordination effectiveness); and third, the ADC emphasizes ecosystem-building as the primary mechanism for creating value, while the WAC relies on the market and the BEC on government interventions.

APPENDIX 7-D, FIGURE D-1. **The ASEAN Development Model**

Embracing the industry 4.0 revolution	Synergy	• Global integration • Government-market interdependence • Domestic economic integration • Whole of government • Sharing economies
	Vigor	• Institutional quality (stability, consistency, transparency, coordination, control of corruption) • Value creation (efficiency, effectiveness, and productivity) • Competitiveness (strategic positioning, turning vulnerabilities to strengths, solution focus, culture) • Factor conditions (infrastructure, entrepreneurship, human capital, financial sector, innovation capacity) • Resilience (pragmatism, discipline, ecosystem)
	Sustainability	• Quality of life • Future-readiness • Resources conservation • Diversity and inclusiveness • Mutual respect and understanding

Source: Khuong Vu, *Economic Catch-up Strategy in the 21st Century: From Concept to Action* (unpublished book manuscript).

APPENDIX 7-D, TABLE D-1. The ASEAN Development Model

Feature	Washington consensus (WAC)	Beijing consensus (BEC)	ASEAN consensus (ADC)
Example	United States	China	Singapore
Primary question	What?	How?	Why?
Strategic objective	Stability and growth	Development	Prosperity
Central priority	Efficiency	Effectiveness	Value creation
Transformative mechanism	Market	Coordination	Ecosystem
Optimization scope	Local	Local	Global
External enablers	No discussion	Globalization	ICT revolution; globalization

Source: Khuong Vu, *Economic Catch-up Strategy in the 21st Century: From Concept to Action* (unpublished book manuscript).

Notes

1. Edward J. Lincoln, "End of the Miracle, Exploring the Asian Financial Crisis" (Washington, DC: The Brookings Institution, June 1, 1998) https://www.brookings .edu/articles/end-of-the-miracle-exploring-the-asian-financial-crisis/.

2. This advantage implies that developing countries that are far from the knowledge frontier can quickly and less riskily adopt knowledge and know-how that have been developed in the advanced nations. See Alexander Gerschenkron, *Economic Backwardness in Historical Perspective: A Book of Essays* (Cambridge: Belknap Press of Harvard University Press, 1962).

3. The industry's ISIC code is 30 (Office, accounting and computing machinery).

4. Andrea Shalal and Heather Timmons, "Fallout from Trump's trade wars felt by economies around the world," Reuters, October 19, 2019, www.reuters.com/ article/us-imf-worldbank-trade/fallout-from-trumps-trade-wars-felt-by-economies -around-the-world-idUSKBN1WY0PZ.

5. The "damage" year is the year when the turbulence is believed to have caused the most severe damage.

6. For a succinct explanation about the VUCA environment, see Jeroen Kraaijenbrink, "What Does VUCA Really Mean?" *Forbes*, December 19, 2018, www .forbes.com/sites/jeroenkraaijenbrink/2018/12/19/what-does-vuca-really-mean/ #478fe8af17d6.

7. The World Bank, *The East Asian Miracle: Economic Growth and Public Policy* (New York: Oxford University Press, 1993); Khuong Vu, *The Dynamics of Economic*

Growth: Policy Insights from Comparative Analyses in Asia (Cheltenham, UK: Edward Elgar Pub, December 2013).

8. Jonathan Stromseth, "Beyond binary choices? Navigating great power competition in Southeast Asia" (Washington, DC: The Brookings Institution, April 2020), https://www.brookings.edu/research/beyond-binary-choices-navigating -great-power-competition-in-southeast-asia/.

9. John Williamson, "What Washington Means by Policy Reform," in *Latin American Adjustment: How Much Has Happened*, ed. John Williamson (Washington, DC: Peterson Institute for International Economics, April 1990), 90–120; Joshua Cooper Ramos, "The Beijing Consensus, Notes on the New Physics of Chinese Power" (London: Foreign Affairs Policy Centre, May 11, 2004), http://www. chinaelections.org/uploadfile/200909/20090918021638239.pdf.

10. Khuong Vu and Kris Hartley, Consensus (Singapore: Ethos, forthcoming).

8

Historical Tensions and Contemporary Governance Challenges in Southeast Asia

The Case of Indonesia

BEN BLAND

INTRODUCTION

Foreign observers of Southeast Asia have long flitted between optimism and despondency when tracking this important region. In the last few years, negativity has been on the rise as key Southeast Asian nations have become embroiled in protracted governance challenges. The five large Southeast Asian nations with fully or partially democratic systems—Indonesia, Malaysia, Myanmar, the Philippines, and Thailand—are all facing profound political and social problems. They seem to be moving in the wrong direction when it comes to key aspects of their economic, social, and democratic development. That is bad news for the United States, Australia, and other Western governments, which have been trying to intensify their engagement with these influential countries, in part as ballast against a rising China.[1]

Analysts and academics have offered a variety of sweeping explanations for this trend, from a global democratic recession to the increasing appeal of China's authoritarian model and from deepening social inequality to the spread of divisive social media platforms. However, using the case of Indonesia, this chapter will argue that it is more instructive to see the problems faced by these countries in their own unique historical context. In particular, this chapter will argue that many of the major governance problems faced by Indonesia—as well as Malaysia, Myanmar, the Philippines, and Thailand—are the result of long-running tensions, which in some cases date back to the late colonial era and the struggle for independence. Rather than seeing these countries as backsliding, we should see them as nations that are still in the making. They are yet to find definitive answers to existential questions such as who controls state power, how the economy is oriented, and who can be a citizen.

Consider Indonesia, Southeast Asia's most populous nation, and its biggest economy. Despite a track record of steady (if unspectacular) economic growth, Indonesia's prospects appear clouded by a combination of weakening democratic governance, social polarization, and confused economic policymaking. These problems, which have been highlighted by Indonesia's patchy response to the ongoing COVID-19 crisis, are often laid at the door of individual political actors or new global trends. However, they are better understood as consequences of three main historical tensions.

First, in terms of politics, Indonesia has developed remarkably resilient, free, and fair elections since the fall of Suharto in 1998. But Indonesia's democracy remains defective in other important respects because of the endurance of Suharto-era elites and institutions, as well as the deep roots of authoritarian and illiberal thinking and practice. Second, in terms of religion, Indonesia is still struggling to find a stable balance in the relationship between Islam and the state, a conundrum that stretches back to its origins as an independent nation in 1945. Third, in terms of economic orientation, Indonesia remains caught between the nationalistic principles established at its foundation and its ever more pressing reliance on foreign funding and technology to maintain growth and job generation.

DEMOCRACY VERSUS AUTHORITARIANISM

Indonesia has developed one of the freest and fairest electoral systems in Southeast Asia. It demonstrated that again in April 2019, when the country pulled off the world's most complicated single-day election with impressive efficiency. But Indonesia's democratic system is increasingly defective in substantive terms.[2] President Joko "Jokowi" Widodo rose from obscurity to national leadership in a few short years thanks to the competitive nature of Indonesian elections—and he was meant to be the outsider who changed the system for the better. Yet, he appears to have succumbed to the system, proving to be a poor guardian of democracy.[3] Six years into his presidency, Jokowi is showing increasing flashes of the authoritarianism that activists believed was in the past.[4]

Jokowi has sought compromises with corrupt politicians and intolerant religious leaders, surrounded himself with former generals with little commitment to democratic principles, and sought to weaken Indonesia's respected anti-corruption agency.[5] On his watch, human rights, the rule of law, and the protection of minorities have all weakened. A decade ago, Rizal Sukma, one of Indonesia's most eminent policy analysts, published a paper arguing that the country's politics were characterized by "defective elections, resilient democracy." Now, Indonesian politics looks more like a story of resilient elections, defective democracy.[6]

Thanks to fiercely competitive elections, the Indonesian people can oust bad leaders and choose better ones. However, they lose much control and accountability in between elections. That can be seen in the "big tent" coalition Jokowi has built in his second term, including his twice-defeated presidential rival Prabowo Subianto, who he appointed as defence minister. The promiscuous power-sharing of Indonesia's post-Suharto presidents, and the concomitant weakness of the formal political opposition, has been characterised as "party cartelization, Indonesian-style."[7] When Jokowi decided to stand for the presidency in 2014, he promised to reject the political horse-trading of his predecessor, Susilo Bambang Yudhoyono, and to build a more targeted and cohesive coalition. However, he quickly abandoned this pledge when confronted by the need to build a political support base.

Although Jokowi has come under sustained criticism for his big-tent Cabinets, his approach reflects a key structural fault in Indonesia's political system as much as a failure of personal resolve. The dominance of personality, patronage, and established political parties, and the lack of political finance reform, has entrenched the power of a small group of elite actors. Many of the challenges to democracy in Indonesia today stem from the "original sin" of *reformasi*, the reform movement that gave birth to the modern Indonesian polity and ensured the ousting of long-ruling autocrat Suharto in 1998. By opting for a process of gradual change from within rather than a revolution, Indonesia avoided the immense bloodshed that would have accompanied efforts to truly dismantle the *ancien régime*. Yet the price of a mostly smooth and peaceful transition has been to leave Suharto-era figures and institutions with a seat at the table of power, from Suharto's Golkar Party to generals with questionable human rights records such as Wiranto and Prabowo. In effect, the rules of the game changed in 1998 but many of the players stayed the same.

The burst of mass student protests across Indonesia in September and October 2019 were a reaction against the enduring power of the elite and its efforts to erode democratic practices and accountability.[8] The students sought, very deliberately, to rekindle the spirit of 1998, and highlight what has been lost since, with their protest slogan *"reformasi dikorupsi"* (reform has been corrupted). However, a more accurate formation might be "reform has never been completed."

The tension between democracy and authoritarianism can be traced to the origins of modern Indonesia. Founding President Sukarno oversaw a brief period of democratic rule in the 1950s. However, within two years of the 1955 legislative elections—Indonesia's first nationwide voting exercise—he became frustrated by the country's divisive politics and took direct control in what he euphemistically called "guided democracy." As well as self-aggrandisement, this reflected Sukarno's philosophical qualms about Western-style liberal democracy, which he argued was ill-suited to Indonesia's collectivist character.

The contemporary academic orthodoxy suggests that Indonesia is one of many countries suffering from a global trend of democratic backsliding. Activists in Indonesia lay the blame for this at Jokowi's feet. But the problem is not that the president has deliberately sought to dismantle Indonesian democracy. Rather, his weak leadership has exposed the resilience of authoritarian actors, thinking, and institutions in Indonesia.

PLURALISM VERSUS MAJORITARIANISM

Religious polarization, which has been intensifying in Indonesia over the last few years, came to a head in last April's bitterly fought presidential and legislative elections. Prabowo tapped support from hard-line Islamist groups and pitched himself as the defender of the faith. Jokowi picked a conservative cleric as his second-term running mate to neutralize criticisms of his commitment to Islam, while his supporters attacked Prabowo for a lack of personal piety. The election results suggested that the vitriol spreading through social media was reflective of real divides. Support for Prabowo surged in conservative Muslim provinces such as Aceh, South Sulawesi, and West Sumatra, while backing for Jokowi jumped among non-Muslims, 97% of whom voted for him according to exit polling by Indikator, a respected survey agency.[9]

Some academics have questioned whether this polarization runs deep in society or if it is more reflective of contingent political factors—including the fact that Indonesia has seen two bitterly opposed candidates facing off against each other directly, or indirectly, in three major election campaigns over the last five years.[10] Jokowi's selection of Prabowo as his defence minister in October seems to support the idea, which was promoted privately by advisers in both camps during the election, that they can deploy identity politics during campaigning but put the religion genie back in the bottle afterward and carry on with business as usual.[11] However, this view exaggerates politicians' ability to manipulate public opinion. Advisers to Prabowo and Jokowi were trying to exploit real religious divides, they did not create them. Indonesian Muslims have become more pious in recent years. However, the divisive debate over the role of Islam in the state—a battle between pluralistic and majoritarian visions—dates to the foundation of Indonesia as an independent nation in 1945.

Indonesia is in an extremely unusual position with regards to its relationship between religion and state. Most Muslim-majority nations fall into three camps. There are full-on Islamic states, such as Iran and Saudi Arabia, which officially position the religion as a driving force behind their existence and their ongoing policy orientation. There are those with Islam as their official religion, such as Malaysia and Pakistan. And then there are secular states such as Senegal and Uzbekistan. The Indonesian state is neither secular nor explicitly Islamic, although it is often mischaracterised as the former and seen to be heading in the direction of the latter. Although nearly 90% of its 270 million people are Muslim, Indonesia has six official religions: Islam, Catholicism, Protestantism, Hinduism, Buddhism, and Confucianism. The constitution allows freedom of worship but says that the state is "based upon the belief in the one and only god."

This compromise was designed to head off efforts to implement Shariah law at Indonesia's foundation in 1945.[12] But it was a very uneasy resolution. From the Darul Islam rebellion that began in 1949, with a mission to turn Indonesia into an Islamic state, to the growing political polarization around religious issues today, this fundamental tension still looms large. It can be seen in the increasing pressure on the political and human rights of religious minorities, from a rise in blasphemy prosecutions to the spread of local Shariah bylaws.[13] Politicians who lack any clear ideological or policy differentiation have increasingly sought to exploit this religious divide as a tool of mobilization, even as Indonesia's Islamic political parties have struggled to increase their combined vote share significantly above 30%.

Jokowi's decision to bring Prabowo and his Great Indonesia Movement Party (Gerindra) into the government, peeling them away from their Islamist camp followers, has cooled some elite political divisions over religion. However, it does not resolve the fundamental struggle for the soul of the Indonesian state.

ECONOMIC NATIONALISM VERSUS THE NEED FOR FOREIGN INVESTMENT

Despite the great potential of Southeast Asia's biggest economy, foreign investors and international development partners have frequently been disappointed in Indonesia. Just when they believe that the government of the day has finally committed to opening up to foreign capital, a policy U-turn suggests that the country is once more falling victim to protectionist forces. While often chalked down to the incompetence or weakness of the leadership, this flip-flopping is better understood as a consequence of a deeper tension between Indonesia's protectionist roots and its need for foreign funding.

Indonesia has many of the trappings of a socialist state, although communism is illegal—and alleged leftists were slaughtered by the hundreds of thousands in the mass killings of the 1960s that were painted as a response to a Communist coup attempt. There is a national planning ministry, price controls on everything from airline flights to off-street car parking, and a large and increasingly influential state-owned enterprise sector. The Indonesian constitution enshrines the need for self-sufficiency and a balance between "progress and unity" in the economy, as well as insisting that key economic sectors and natural resources are "controlled by the state."[14]

However, after Western-trained economic technocrats (the so-called Berkeley Mafia) ascended to influential positions under Suharto's leadership from the late 1960s onward, Indonesia started to liberalize its economy and bring in foreign capital and technology to generate growth and ensure political stability. Today, as Jokowi watches rapid growth in neighbouring countries such as Vietnam with envy, Indonesia is still looking to foreign investors to fill the gap, in terms of both capital and expertise. But, while Jokowi promises to open the economy, he has simultaneously presided over a major push to deepen the role of state-owned enterprises. He has also overseen a broad program of nationalization, which has moved some of the country's biggest resource projects (including the large mines previously controlled by U.S. companies Freeport and Newmont and a major gas block operated by France's Total) into state control.

This parallel push for foreign capital and state control of the economy confuses many investors. And this approach certainly leads to some confounding results in international measures of competitiveness. In his first term, Jokowi released round after round of supposed deregulation packages that were meant to make the country more attractive for foreign investors. And, on his watch, Indonesia surged up the World Bank's closely watched "ease of doing business" ranking from 120th to 73rd place.[15] But despite some permitting processes being streamlined and some foreign investment limits being reduced, it is hard to find foreign investors who believe that it has got any easier to do business in practice. They still complain about the same structural problems: corruption, red tape, disjointed governance, weak rule of law, and protectionist impulses across the government. Despite the World Bank ranking improvement, Indonesia's regulatory regime for foreign direct investment is one of the most restrictive of the sixty-eight middle- and lower-middle-income countries assessed in a recent survey by the Organisation for Economic Co-operation and Development.[16]

However, as with identity politics and the concerns about democratic backsliding, Indonesia's economic tensions are as much the result of unresolved historical tensions as they are the result of contemporary personality and policy questions. Politicians promote protectionist policies—and rent-seeking tycoons, politicians, and officials exploit this approach—because there is genuine public support for, and a constitutional commitment to, a more protectionist economy. Investors hoping for a liberal Indonesia that embraces foreign investment will be in a for a very long wait.

AS INDONESIA BATTLES COVID-19, DEEPER CONFLICTS PERSIST

The COVID-19 pandemic is an unforgiving test of states' governing capacity and the agility of their political leaders. Indonesia is not faring well, with a rising case load and a government that has failed to set out a clear strategy for tackling the twin health and economic crises.[17] Part of the problem is a lack of capacity in the health system and the government more generally.[18] But the crisis has also highlighted some of the long-standing tensions discussed in this chapter.

While often disregarding experts in public health and epidemiology, Jokowi has looked to the military and the police to lead the response to COVID-19.[19] This approach reveals the enduring power of the military, more than two decades after the post-Suharto reforms that ended its "dual function" role in civilian government. It also underlines the persistence of authoritarian figures and authoritarian thinking in the Indonesian government. The president is not actively trying to roll back democracy. But he is reaching for the levers of power that he thinks will get him quick results, and in doing so has highlighted the limits of *reformasi*.

Remarkably, the ideological conflict over the role of Islam has also persisted at this time of crisis. In the midst of the pandemic, Jokowi's Indonesia Democratic Party of Struggle (PDI-P) was busy pushing a bill to promote the national ideology of *Pancasila*, which was invented by Sukarno, the father of PDI-P chair Megawati Sukarnoputri.[20] The five abstract principles of *Pancasila*—belief in one god, a just and civilized humanity, the unity of Indonesia, democracy guided by collective wisdom, and social justice—were designed as a compromise between nationalists such as Sukarno and Islamists who wanted Shariah law enshrined in the Indonesian constitution. The bill, which may have been intended as a sop to Megawati, prompted a backlash from Islamists who argued that it was designed to dilute the religious character of *Pancasila*. Facing determined opposition, Jokowi's government dropped the bill. But the row highlighted the enduring potency of this fundamental dispute at the heart of the Indonesian state.

Similarly, on the economic front, the pandemic has reinforced the tension between Indonesia's need for foreign capital and its desire for self-sufficiency. In response to the crisis, Jokowi's government has emphasised the need to intensify the domestic production of key medical and pharmaceutical products, as well as foodstuffs. At the same time, however, it has expressed a desire to attract more foreign investment, as the economy heads for its worst crunch since the Asian financial crisis in 1997–1998.[21] With such contradictory aims, it is little wonder that Indonesia is facing mounting difficulties. Part of the problem is poor leadership from the president and his Cabinet.[22] But even a much more strategic and decisive leader would struggle because of the deep-seated structural problems discussed in this chapter.

CONCLUSION AND RECOMMENDATIONS

Some analysts interpret the political, religious, and economic tensions outlined above as failures of leadership by Jokowi and those around him. Others tend to situate them in the context of global trends, whether it be democratic recession, rising protectionism or technology-driven polarization. However, this chapter argues that Indonesia's biggest challenges emanate to a great extent from unresolved questions about what sort of nation it should be. Less than seventy-five years have passed since Indonesia was jolted into existence as an improbable nation forged out of the arbitrary territorial limits of Dutch colonial expansion. So it is not surprising that Indonesia is still a nation in the making. And it is far from alone in the region in its struggle to answer existential questions about how to orient its politics, economy, and society.

In Malaysia, a reformist opposition coalition won power in 2018 for the first time ever. But it fell apart in less than two years as it struggled to overcome personality disputes and the fraught, interlinked problems of race, religion, and economic inequality.[23] In Thailand, the decades-long battle between the monarchy, the military, and those who want democracy looks no closer to a stable resolution, despite the junta eventually coming out on top in a heavily manipulated electoral process last year.[24] In Myanmar, an election is due in November 2020 but it is unlikely to offer any clear path forward on the fundamental questions of how the military shares power with civilians and how to forge a united, peaceful nation from the country's disparate ethnic groups and myriad conflicts.[25] And in the Philippines, President Rodrigo Duterte's disturbing leadership reflects deep faults within the country's politics, from the primacy of personalistic leadership and the dominance of dynasties to the weaknesses of democratic institutions.[26]

The depth of these domestic challenges should be a concern for the United States and Australia as they hope to deepen engagement with Southeast Asia. Countries embroiled in existential crises are not likely to step up in tackling regional challenges. However, Western governments should not succumb to resignation in the face of these seemingly intractable problems. Rather, they need to better understand the historical roots of Southeast Asia's contemporary governance issues, to craft their assistance accordingly, and to settle in for a long ride as these countries grapple with delicate and long-standing questions of nation-building.

They should:

■ **Be ambitious but realistic.** Expectations of Indonesia have risen to the point where disappointment is likely to set in. Western officials regularly talk of Indonesia as an economic powerhouse and an emerging great power in Asia. But Indonesia is facing a series of enduring, fundamental challenges that are unlikely to be resolved anytime soon. By setting the bar so high, there is a risk of rapid disillusionment. The United States, Australia, and other Western nations are right to be ambitious about their relationships with Indonesia. But they need to understand that Indonesia is still a nation in the making. They should temper their rhetoric and work harder with Indonesia on solving today's practical problems. Outsiders cannot force Indonesia to be more democratic, economically liberal, or religiously tolerant. But they can help it to become a more resilient, effective, and equitable country.

■ **Deepen cooperation with civil society in Indonesia.** Western leaders are fond of calling Indonesia a beacon of democracy in Asia and the Muslim world. But this phrase glosses over the real challenges facing Indonesian democracy today, and the enduring power of authoritarian thinking and authoritarian actors. Western governments need to acknowledge this fragile reality and work more with civil society groups in Indonesia. In recent years more development funding has gone straight to government and some of this needs to be re-directed to strengthen NGOs, which were already struggling financially before the pandemic hit. The focus should not be on "democracy-building" per se but supporting the wide range of groups that are working to build a fairer, more transparent and accountable country, whether by boosting women's economic empowerment or exposing corruption and environmental degradation.

■ **Engage with Indonesia in its own right, not as a part of plan to counterbalance China.** There is an increasing tendency for security analysts in Washington, Canberra, and other Western capitals to see the relationship with Indonesia and other Southeast Asian nations through the lens of competition with China. This is a mistake. As it struggles with the profound historical tensions outlined above, Indonesia sees its biggest challenges coming from the inside, not the outside. Jakarta's deep commitment to a nonaligned foreign policy is specifically designed to prevent external conflicts from reopening old wounds in the Indonesia body politic. The best way to get closer to Indonesia is to help it tackle its domestic challenges, not to push it to take on an international role with which it is not comfortable.

Notes

1. Jonathan Stromseth and Hunter Marston, "Democracy at a crossroads in Southeast Asia: Great power rivalry meets domestic governance" (Washington, DC: The Brookings Institution, February 2019), https://www.brookings.edu/research/political-trends-in-southeast-asia-great-power-rivalry-meets-domestic-governance/.

2. Ben Bland, "Politics in Indonesia: Resilient elections, defective democracy" (Sydney: Lowy Institute, April 10, 2019), https://www.lowyinstitute.org/publications/politics-indonesia-resilient-elections-defective-democracy.

3. I expand on this argument in my forthcoming book *Man of Contradictions: Joko Widodo and the Struggle to Remake Indonesia* (New York: Penguin Random House, 2020).

4. Thomas P. Power, "Jokowi's Authoritarian Turn and Indonesia's Democratic Decline," *Bulletin of Indonesian Economic Studies* 54, no. 3 (December 2018): 307–338, https://doi.org/10.1080/00074918.2018.1549918.

5. Eve Warburton and Edward Aspinall, "Explaining Indonesia's Democratic Regression: Structure, Agency and Popular Opinion," *Contemporary Southeast Asia* 41, no. 2 (August 2019): 255-285, https://muse.jhu.edu/article/732138.

6. Rizal Sukma, "Indonesian politics in 2009: defective elections, resilient democracy," *Bulletin of Indonesian Economic Studies* 45, no. 3 (November 2009): 317–336, https://doi.org/10.1080/00074910903301647.

7. Dan Slater, "Party Cartelization, Indonesian-Style: Presidential Power

-Sharing and the Contingency of Democratic Opposition," *Journal of East Asian Studies* 18, no. 1 (March 2018): 23–46, https://doi.org/10.1017/jea.2017.26.

8. Max Walden, "Students dead, activists arrested amid protests to stop legal changes in Indonesia," ABC News (Australia), October 2, 2019, https://www.abc.net .au/news/2019-10-02/students-dead-activists-arrested-amid-protests-in-indonesia/ 11561714.

9. "NU, non-Muslim voters held 'key role' in Jokowi's win," *The Jakarta Post*, July 25, 2019, https://www.thejakartapost.com/news/2019/07/25/nu-non-muslim -voters-held-key-role-jokowi-s-win.html.

10. Eve Warburton, "Polarisation in Indonesia: what if perception is reality?" New Mandala, April 16, 2019, https://www.newmandala.org/how-polarised-is -indonesia/.

11. Author interview with Eve Warburton, Jakarta, April 2019.

12. R. E. Elson, "Another Look at the Jakarta Charter Controversy of 1945," Indonesia, no. 88 (October 2009): 105-130, https://www.jstor.org/stable/40376487.

13. Andreas Harsono, "Indonesia to Expand Abusive Blasphemy Law," Human Rights Watch, October 31, 2019, https://www.hrw.org/news/2019/10/31/indonesia -expand-abusive-blasphemy-law.

14. Hal Hill and Deasy Pane, "Indonesia and the Global Economy: Missed Opportunities?" in *Indonesia in the New World: Globalisation, Nationalism and Sovereignty*, eds. Arianto A. Patunru, Mari Pangestu and M. Chatib Basri (Singapore: ISEAS Publishing, 2018), 272.

15. "Doing Business 2019" (Washington, DC: The World Bank, October 2018), https://www.doingbusiness.org/en/reports/global-reports/doing-business-2019.

16. "Indonesia Economic Quarterly: Strengthening Competitiveness" (Washington, DC: The World Bank, December 2018), https://www.worldbank.org/en/ country/indonesia/publication/indonesia-economic-quarterly-december-2018.

17. James Massola, "Indonesia set to become third virus hotspot in Asia, expert warns," *Sydney Morning Herald*, July 6, 2020, https://www.smh.com.au/world/asia/ indonesia-set-to-become-third-virus-hot-spot-in-asia-expert-warns-20200706 -p559hi.html.

18. Yanuar Nugroho and Siwage Dharma Negara, "Urgent Need to Strengthen State Capacity: Learning from Indonesia's COVID-19 Crisis" (Singapore: ISEAS - Yusof Ishak Institute, June 19, 2020), https://www.iseas.edu.sg/wp-content/uploads /2020/05/ISEAS_Perspective_2020_66.pdf.

19. Tangguh Chairil, "Indonesia Needs to Change Its Security-Heavy Approach to COVID-19," *The Diplomat*, April 30, 2020, https://thediplomat.com/2020/04/ indonesia-needs-to-change-its-security-heavy-approach-to-covid-19/.

20. Abdurrachman Satrio, "Indonesia's obsession with ideology: the case of the Pancasila bill," Indonesia at Melbourne, The University of Melbourne, July 13, 2020, https://indonesiaatmelbourne.unimelb.edu.au/indonesias-obsession-with-ideology -the-case-of-the-pancasila-bill/.

21. Aris Aditya, "Virus Hit on Indonesia Worse Than Financial Crisis, Jokowi Says," Bloomberg, June 19, 2020, https://www.bloomberg.com/news/articles/2020 -06-19/virus-hit-on-indonesia-worse-than-financial-crisis-jokowi-says.

22. Ben Bland, "Indonesia: Covid-19 crisis reveals cracks in Jokowi's ad hoc politics," The Lowy Institute, March 17, 2020, https://www.lowyinstitute.org/the -interpreter/indonesia-covid-19-crisis-reveals-cracks-jokowi-s-ad-hoc-politics.

23. Liew Chin Tong, "The Great Reset (Part 1) – Resetting Malaysian Politics," Liew Chin Tong, July 3, 2020, https://www.liewchintong.com/2020/07/03/the-great -reset-part-1-resetting-malaysian-politics/.

24. Thitinan Pongsudhirak, "Five years backwards under military rule," *Bangkok Post*, May 24, 2019, https://www.bangkokpost.com/opinion/opinion/1682868/5 -years-backwards-under-military-rule.

25. Mary Callahan and Myo Zaw Oo, "Myanmar's 2020 Elections and Conflict Dynamics" (Washington, DC: United States Institute of Peace, April 2019), https:// www.usip.org/publications/2019/04/myanmars-2020-elections-and-conflict -dynamics.

26. David G. Timberman, "Philippine Politics Under Duterte: A Midterm Assessment" (Washington, DC: Carnegie Endowment for International Peace, January 10, 2019), https://carnegieendowment.org/2019/01/10/philippine-politics -under-duterte-midterm-assessment-pub-78091.

9

Decoupling Governance and Democracy

The Challenge of Authoritarian Development in Southeast Asia

THOMAS PEPINSKY

INTRODUCTION

This chapter provides a panoramic overview of governance trends in Southeast Asia. Descriptively, there are two main findings. First, there is no evidence of region-wide democratic erosion in Southeast Asia in either the short or medium term. Second, we see little correspondence between democratic practices and civil liberties in the region, on one hand, and effective and capable governance, on the other. Governance in Southeast Asia has changed only gradually, these changes have had little to do with changes in formal political institutions such as democratization. These findings have implications for understanding how the so-called Beijing model of authoritarian capitalism—where the state plays an active role in directing economic development in the broader national interest, with a pragmatic emphasis on results rather than ideology, but liberal democratic freedoms are suppressed in the name of political stability—is shaping the region. In the midst of the ongoing COVID-19 pandemic, linked inextricably with China, the question of what sorts of governments are best able to manage pressing large-scale social problems is particularly relevant. These findings also provide useful insights about the possibility and the value of fostering more accountable and effective governments across the region.

Before proceeding it is important to fix terminology. By democracy, I mean the institutional structures and practices that enable meaningful electoral competition between political parties over who may hold legitimate political authority.[1] By governance, I mean the institutional structures practices through which those who hold political power exercise that authority.[2] Democracy and governance are not the same thing, both conceptually (as many have argued) and empirically (as I will show below). It is possible that democratic politics produces more effective and responsible governance,[3] which is one argument for pressing for democratic reforms. It is also possible—as some admirers of the contemporary Chinese approach to capitalism and development hold—that democracy is inimical to effective and responsive governance, or that it is not the right political formation for countries who are facing steep challenges of economic development or political stability. Internally, few countries in Southeast Asia hold that they are anything other than "democratic" (although their understanding of that term varies enormously), and all governments across the region claim to prioritize effective and responsible governance. Before digging into the relationships between governance and democracy and their implications, however, I summarize the empirical record across the region.

QUANTITATIVE TRENDS IN DEMOCRACY AND GOVERNANCE

The basic trends in Southeast Asian democracy are summarized in Figure 9-1, using data compiled by Freedom House in its annual "Freedom in the World" reports.[4] Each line is the sum of Freedom House's "civil liberties" and "political rights" indicators, with higher values corresponding to more freedom (measured in ways that convey, essentially, more democracy).

The first plot in the upper-left-hand corner shows the average composite Freedom House scores for all eleven countries in Southeast Asia (these are raw averages, not weighted by country population). There is no evidence of regression in political rights or civil liberties across the region in

FIGURE 9-1. **Democracy in Southeast Asia, 2001–Present**

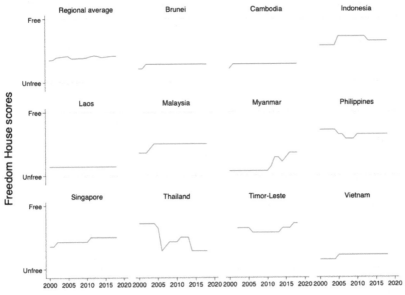

Source: "Freedom in the World," Freedom House.

recent years. The country plots show why: cases of democratic regression such as Thailand have been matched by cases of opening and liberalization (however halting and incomplete) in Myanmar and Timor-Leste. Most countries have remained stable over time. The region's best hope for democracy over the past decade—Indonesia—saw its scores deteriorate early this decade. With the benefit of a bit of perspective, we remember that most country watchers had long expressed their concerns about democratic consolidation and the protection of civil liberties in Southeast Asia.

This conclusion sits at odds with academic analyses and popular discussions about democratic backsliding across the world. For example, the 2018 "Freedom in the World" report's subtitle is "Democracy in Crisis" and its discussion of the Asia-Pacific region references Cambodian Prime Minister's Hun Sen's "crackdown on the country's beleaguered opposition and press corps," as well as the Rohingya genocide and the "military['s] enormous autonomy and political power" in Myanmar.[5] It might also have referenced Philippines President Rodrigo Duterte's vicious anti-drug war, a military-run election in Thailand, concerns about freedom of conscience in Indonesia, and many others.[6] There can be no doubt that these are worrying signs for the fate of democracy in the region. But these concerns are not new, they are simply the latest iterations of medium-term political processes specific to each country.

To summarize trends in governance across the region, Figure 9-2 plots four indicators from the World Bank's Worldwide Governance Indicators dataset.[7] These indicators include corruption, rule of law, government effectiveness, and regulatory quality, each of which reflects a facet of governance or politics other than simply regime type or level of democracy or freedom.

Once again, the upper-left-hand figure plots average levels of governance, and provides little evidence of broad changes in governance across the region. But strikingly, across countries and indicators, we also see little change in governance quality over the past two decades. Countries such as Indonesia and Laos have slowly trended upward, but not by much. Governance indicators for Thailand remain roughly constant, despite truly dramatic political change on multiple occasions. Those countries that scored well on governance indicators in the early 2000s are exactly those who score well today. Only Myanmar has seen meaningful change over time,

FIGURE 9-2. **Governance in Southeast Asia, 2001–Present**

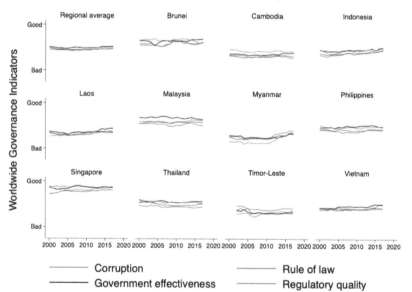

Source: "Worldwide Governance Indicators," The World Bank, https://info.worldbank.org/governance/wgi/.

with regulatory quality improving alongside political liberalization (but no noticeable improvement in government effectiveness or the rule of law). These trends, together, indicate that Southeast Asia as a region is characterized by a *decoupling of governance and regime type.* There is little systematic evidence that democracy is associated with the quality of governance however measured, either in *levels* (Singapore and Brunei score high on governance, much lower on freedom and democracy) or in *changes* (democratic progress in Timor-Leste is not associated with improved governance, and democratic regress in Thailand is not associated with deteriorating governance). Although in a global sample it is true that democracy (or democratization) is associated with good (or improving) governance (see Figure 9-3), the Southeast Asian experience provides no evidence in favor of that proposition.

It is important not to push these conclusions too far. The governance

FIGURE 9-3. **Democracy and Governance around the World**

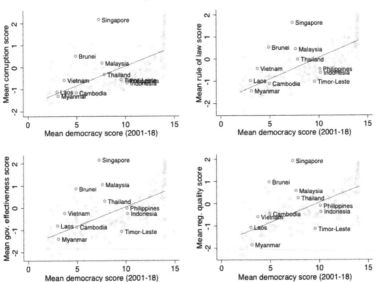

Note: In each chart, each dot represents one of 197 independent countries, with Freedom House democracy scores and Worldwide Governance Indicators averaged between 2001 and the most recent year for which data is available. The labeled red dots locate the Southeast Asian cases.

Source: "Freedom in the World," Freedom House; "Worldwide Governance Indicators," The World Bank.

indicators used here have been subject to abundant critique, with some arguing that they simply proxy for economic development.[8] Indeed, the correlation is quite strong between these governance indicators and levels of economic development, and Southeast Asian cases fall right as they should (see Figure 9-4).

Whether or not the relationship between governance and growth is causal (good governance causes good economic performance) or incidental (good governance is just an imperfect proxy of economic development), the important conclusion is that democracy and governance are decoupled in Southeast Asia.

FIGURE 9-4. **Growth and Governance around the World**

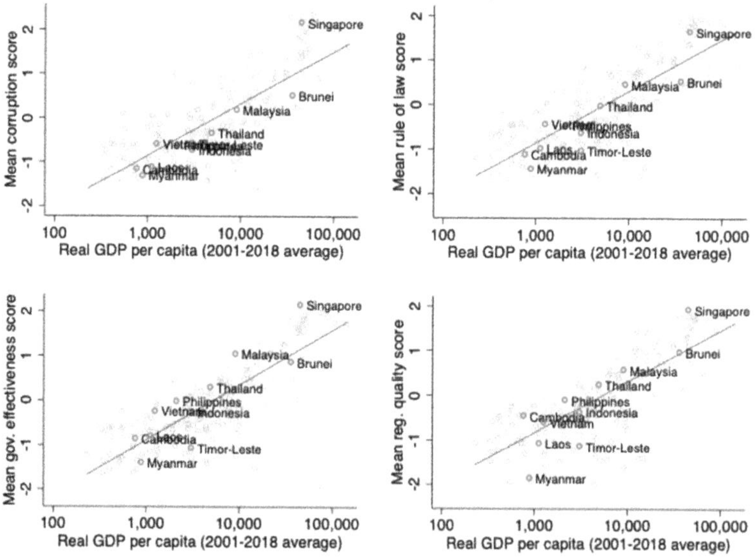

Note: In each chart, each dot represents one of 197 independent countries, with Worldwide Governance Indicators and World Bank data on real GDP per capita in 2010 U.S. dollars, averaged between 2001 and the most recent year for which data is available. The labeled red dots locate the Southeast Asian cases.

Source: "Worldwide Governance Indicators," The World Bank; "World Development Indicators," The World Bank, https://datacatalog.worldbank.org/dataset/world-development-indicators.

LEARNING FROM DECOUPLING

Stepping back, that finding alone is a victory for proponents of authoritarian capitalism and the "Beijing model" or "Beijing Consensus."[9] Democracy's defenders must mount a positive argument that democracy fosters good governance and accountability, and that democracy does not threaten social, economic, or political stability. For those who disagree, it merely suffices to observe that "it depends" or "not necessarily."

But we should not conclude that this offers too much support for Beijing's own understanding of the Chinese growth experience as resting on an exportable political model. Instead, it has long been the case that observers both within and outside the region debate the political foundations of Southeast Asia's economic prosperity. Singapore's development since independence has done more than China's growth since 1978 to establish that, in point of fact, there is no simple correlation between democracy and effective governance under stable legal institutions.[10] This is true even for those observers who recognize the importance of informal institutions rather than some objective and apolitical rule of law in explaining Singapore's success.[11] The governance records of Indonesia and the Philippines since democratization, which have proven disappointing in the years since the 1997 Asian financial crisis undermined the Asian development model, have also undermined any simple argument that democracy produces effective governance.[12] Simply put, the authoritarian development model is an old debate within Southeast Asia.

Nevertheless, we do observe a common emphasis across the region on a relatively small set of issues in economic development, construed as a technocratic or managerial problem rather than a broader political one. In countries as diverse as Vietnam, Myanmar, and Indonesia, regimes champion government effectiveness through delivery of services, infrastructure development, bureaucratic responsiveness, and carefully managed global economic integration. Almost no government opposes these things, regardless of its level of development, history of openness (autarky versus international engagement), political regime (communist single-party state, liberalizing former junta, or electoral democracy). But to reiterate, governance in these contexts is conceived as a technocratic or managerial problem, rather than one of politics, representation, or accountability except for in the vaguest of senses. And both rhetorically and in actual practice, such discourses of governance as a matter of responsiveness and effective administration deemphasize political liberties, freedom of expression, and criticism. Of course, liberal, progressive, and populist voices throughout the region defend civil liberties and civil rights, but they find themselves doing so from outside the halls of power rather than setting the governance agenda from within.

What is the role of China in these developments? Is China strengthening the case for authoritarian capitalism in Southeast Asia, either directly or indirectly? China's economic policies and diplomatic actions do not, to my knowledge, directly encourage authoritarian capitalism or incentivize countries to follow a particular national political or economic model. China has no direct interest in other Southeast Asian countries adopting its political-economic model. Instead, China's primary objective for countries within the region is to establish and maintain regional dominance, which is best accomplished by working with governments of any type within the region and pushing for issues in China's strategic interest (that is, megaprojects, dams, and deference to the Chinese position on the South China Sea).

However, the indirect effects of China's rise are inescapable for politicians and mass publics alike. The very fact of China's rapid economic growth, its successful harnessing of infrastructure and technology to increase material prosperity without creating mass social disorder, means that China is an example to which those dissatisfied with their incumbent regimes can look. Likewise, China's success in managing economic transformation without political liberalization may undermine liberal reformers who press for deeper democracy in Southeast Asia. China's delayed response to COVID-19 illustrates for many the problems of China's political model, with local officials' unwillingness to face the magnitude of pandemic until it was far too late.[13] But others draw attention to how effective China was in stamping out the virus, whereas the United States has fared dismally in comparison.

At the same time, China's position as the regional hegemon (sorry, my fellow Americans) and therefore either a strategic rival (for Indonesia or Thailand) or direct security threat (for Myanmar or Vietnam) places inherent limits on its ability to model capitalist development for the rest of the region.[14] And although popular commentary in Southeast Asia is muted on issues such as the Hong Kong protests and the treatment of

China's minorities in Tibet and Xinjiang, the strategy of hard authoritarian control employed by President Xi Jinping is plain to observers in the region. China's material development and ability to project power are attractive in Southeast Asia, but not so much the politics of the Xi regime. A move to explicitly promote China's political model as one to be adopted by other countries—one that provide carrots to entice governments in the region to adopt China's political structure rather than to act in its diplomatic and economic interests—would amount to a fundamental challenge to Western interests.

ENGAGING SOUTHEAST ASIA

Given these cross-national patterns, historical legacies, sticky institutional trajectories, and the challenges of pressing for meaningful political change, what should be the priority for those who wish to engage with Southeast Asia, fostering democratic practices and more accountable governance? Rather than trying to "re-couple" democracy and accountability within Southeast Asia, on the hypothesis that one will produce the other, a better approach is to acknowledge their decoupling and treat each as a separate issue worthy of pursuit in its own right.

This means, first and foremost, a narrow focus on what accountable governance might mean in less-than-democratic settings. Southeast Asia's authoritarian regimes vary in their ability and willingness to anticipate the needs and concerns of key stakeholders at home. But both within the region and without, a more open economic development model requires these regimes to liberalize their domestic political economies to some degree. Contrast Myanmar under autarky with Myanmar since liberalization, or Indonesia prior to the 1980s deregulatory push and Indonesia afterward. There is no need to argue that such liberalization produces truly meaningful political accountability or progressive and inclusive pro-poor policies, but it does create incentives for governments to develop procedures to anticipate the needs of at least some important economic and social sectors. To take one prominent example, Vietnam's opening since the late 1980s has spurred a range of institutional reforms at the subnational level, which have been matched with efforts to assess institutional quality (as proxied through competitiveness), which may indeed have been strengthened by increasing openness.[15] Foreign donors have played a central role in these efforts.[16] Vietnam is not a democracy, and those left behind by development have only limited access to the ears of policymakers in Hanoi, but local governance has improved nevertheless, and the country's political economy has been transformed as a result. And indeed, Vietnam's enviable record of managing COVID-19 illustrates how such transparency-enhancing reforms can have enormous social and economic benefits.[17]

Separately, one might strengthen democratic practices by recognizing that they are valuable in their own right. That is, rather than mounting an argument that democracy produces accountability and effective governance, defend democracy as a process and mechanism through which to support individual rights, liberties, and freedoms. These matter, and they may be improved even under regimes that do not oversee meaningfully competitive elections, or even when they do not improve governance outcomes in electoral democracies. Singapore may permit greater levels of public protest without disturbing the People's Action Party's rule much at all; the Philippines may halt extrajudicial killings of suspected drug dealers without threatening the regular rotation of family dynasties in that country's politics; Laos may loosen its grip on the press without undermining the Lao People's Revolutionary Party's grip on power; and the Rohingya may be saved from genocide without upsetting the delicate balance of power between the army and the National League for Democracy in Myanmar. Although the empirical record does not support the proposition that democracy or civil liberties create good governance and economic growth, there is little evidence either that increasing political rights and civil liberties within Southeast Asia has undermined good governance or prevented economic development either (which is another conclusion that one may draw from Figure 2 above).

But do these values conflict? In other words, does protecting individuals' ability to claim rights and exercise liberties undermine accountability or effectiveness, perhaps by making governing "too hard" or opening up politics to what Indonesia's anti-democratic first president, Sukarno, dismissed as "free fight liberalism" characterized by competition among many pressure groups seeking influence and ethnic minorities exerting disproportionate political power?[18] Once again, there is no need to deny that authoritarian control suppresses the challenges associated with representative government; that is, after all, one of the main arguments in favor of limiting civil liberties and mobilizing state power under the Beijing model. But it is hard to conclude that Indonesia's and the Philippines' central development challenges are that their citizens have too many rights. Indonesia's slow response to COVID-19 and the challenging policymaking environment for a country with insufficient public health infrastructure both are problems of governance,[19] not of political rights and civil liberties.

The policy implications that follow from this discussion are straightforward.

■ **The international donor community should prioritize reforms that target efficiency and capacity.** Consistent with a long history of development policymaking and the priorities of the international donor community, external supporters of democratic liberties and accountable government can press for greater economic openness across the region without making these efforts conditional on democratic reforms. Those who press for more effective government may look for points of common agreement with their counterparts: the importance of clear regulatory frameworks, dispute-resolution procedures, employee rights and voice, and data transparency.

■ **Watch what lessons are drawn from COVID-19—and who draws them.** The American and Chinese experiences with COVID-19 are different, but what they share is that they expose weaknesses in both Beijing's and Washington's ability to handle fast-moving pandemics. Each country's leadership is keen to steer the narrative. A key point to watch is whether Southeast Asian countries focus on the narrative of culpability (U.S. President Donald Trump's obsession) or the narrative of effective management (Xi Jinping's focus). Even if Southeast Asia's governments express more frustration with China's slow movement to contain the pandemic in early 2020, mass publics and oppositions may be more attuned to the effectiveness of China's eventual response.[20] As conditions continue to worsen in the United States (as of July 2020), the Trump administration's catastrophic mismanagement of the American public health response will further undermine the U.S. position in Southeast Asia.

■ **Reforms that target local governments may be less politically objectionable than reforms that target national political institutions.** Reform efforts that target accountability and transparency focus on improving local governance and government capacity at the subnational level while remaining mindful of the difficulties of changing national political institutions and modes of government through anything other than slow, deliberate, patient work. That few governments are explicitly opposed to such these kinds of efforts, at least in broad strokes, means that there are many opportunities for engagement.

■ **Supporters of deeper democracy and greater civil liberties should not base their arguments on the presumed economic benefits of democracy.** At the same time, work on civil liberties may resist the temptation the portray the protection of civil rights and political liberties in economic consequentialist terms, especially in imperfect democracies such as Indonesia and the Philippines. The better argument is that Southeast Asians desire democratic rights for the same reason that people around the world desire them: because they provide voice (if not necessarily accountability or responsiveness) and as a result allow citizens to advocate for their own civil liberties. The work that many governments and nongovernmental organizations do to support the right to protest, access to information, freedom of the press, and freedom of conscience is invaluable, even if it does not always generate the desired outcomes. And unlike governance trends which are sticky, rights and liberties do change over time, so there are grounds for optimism.

Notes

1. An accessible summary discussion is Philippe C. Schmitter and Terry Lynn Karl, "What Democracy Is . . . And Is Not," *Journal of Democracy* 2, no. 3 (Summer 1991): 3–16, https://www.ned.org/docs/Philippe-C-Schmitter-and-Terry-Lynn-Karl -What-Democracy-is-and-Is-Not.pdf.

2. On "good" governance, see Bo Rothstein and Jan Teorell, "What Is Quality of Government? A Theory of Impartial Government Institutions," *Governance* 21, no. 2 (April 2008): 165–190, https://doi.org/10.1111/j.1468-0491.2008.00391.x.

3. See Alícia Adserà, Carles Boix, and Mark Payne, "Are You Being Served? Political Accountability and Quality of Government," *Journal of Law, Economics, and Organization* 19, no. 2 (2003): 445–490, https://doi.org/10.1093/jleo/ewg017.

4. "Freedom in the World," Freedom House, https://freedomhouse.org/report/ freedom-world. There are few differences if I use the Center for Systemic Peace's Polity Project scores; see "The Polity Project," Center for Systemic Peace, https:// www.systemicpeace.org/polityproject.html.

5. Michael J. Abramowitz, "Freedom in the World 2018: Democracy in Crisis,"

(Washington, DC: Freedom House, 2018), 14, https://freedomhouse.org/sites/default/files/2020-02/FH_FIW_Report_2018_Final.pdf.

6. See Thomas B. Pepinsky, "Southeast Asia: Voting Against Disorder," *Journal of Democracy* 28, no. 2 (April 2017): 120–131, https://muse.jhu.edu/article/653381.

7. "Worldwide Governance Indicators," The World Bank, https://info.worldbank.org/governance/wgi/.

8. See Marcus J. Kurtz and Andrew Schrank, "Growth and Governance: Models, Measures, and Mechanisms," *Journal of Politics* 69, no. 2 (May 2007): 538–554, https://doi.org/10.1111/j.1468-2508.2007.00549.x.

9. For discussions, see Stefan Halper, *The Beijing Consensus: How China's Authoritarian Model Will Dominate the Twenty-First Century* (New York: Basic Books, 2010); Yasheng Huang, "Rethinking the Beijing Consensus," *Asia Policy* 11 (January 2011): 1–26, https://muse.jhu.edu/article/413017.

10. Singapore has had particular influence on the Asian development model; see Fareed Zakaria, "Culture Is Destiny: A Conversation with Lee Kuan Yew," *Foreign Affairs* 73, no. 2 (1994), https://www.foreignaffairs.com/articles/asia/1994-03-01/conversation-lee-kuan-yew-0. It is even proven influential for China itself; see Stephan Ortmann, "The 'Beijing consensus' and the 'Singapore model': unmasking the myth of an alternative authoritarian state-capitalist model," *Journal of Chinese Economic and Business Studies* 10, no. 4 (2012): 337–359, https://doi.org/10.1080/14765284.2012.724981.

11. See Natasha Hamilton-Hart, "The Singapore state revisited," *Pacific Review* 13, no. 2 (2000): 195-216, https://doi.org/10.1080/095127400363550.

12. Mark R. Thompson, "Pacific Asia after 'Asian Values': Authoritarianism, Democracy, and 'Good Governance'," *Third World Quarterly* 25, no. 6 (2004): 1079–1095, https://www.jstor.org/stable/3993752.

13. Yuen Yuen Ang, "When COVID-19 meets centralized, personalized power," *Nature Human Behaviour* 4, no. 5 (April 9, 2020): 445–447, https://www.nature.com/articles/s41562-020-0872-3.

14. The possible exception is for Cambodia, China's most pliable partner in the region.

15. See Duc Anh Dang, "How foreign direct investment promote institutional quality: Evidence from Vietnam," *Journal of Comparative Economics* 41, no. 4 (November 2013): 1054–1072, https://www.sciencedirect.com/science/article/pii/S0147596713000863.

16. Jonathan Stromseth, "Good Governance and International Development Cooperation," in "Emerging Asian Approaches to Development Cooperation" (Seoul: Korea Development Institute and The Asia Foundation, 2011), 100–102, https://asiafoundation.org/resources/pdfs/EmergingAsianApproachestoDevelopmentCooperationConferencePapers.pdf.

17. Trang (Mae) Nguyen and Edmund J. Malesky, "Reopening Vietnam: How the country's improving governance helped it weather the COVID-19 pandemic," The Brookings Institution, May 20, 2020, https://www.brookings.edu/blog/order-from-chaos/2020/05/20/reopening-vietnam-how-the-countrys-improving-governance-helped-it-weather-the-covid-19-pandemic/.

18. On these concerns in the context of liberalizing political control, see M. Hadi Soesastro, "The Political Economy of Deregulation in Indonesia," *Asian Survey* 29, no. 9 (September 1989): 853–869, https://www.jstor.org/stable/2644831.

19. Jeffrey Neilson, "Without social safety nets, Indonesia risks political instability over COVID-19," New Mandala, April 22, 2020, https://www.newmandala.org/indonesia-risks-political-instability-over-covid-19/.

20. For more on the US-China competition over COVID-19 in Southeast Asia, see Jonathan Stromseth, "U.S.-China rivalry after COVID-19: Clues and early indications from Southeast Asia," The Brookings Institution, May 14, 2020, https://www.brookings.edu/blog/order-from-chaos/2020/05/14/us-china-rivalry-after-covid-19-clues-and-early-indications-from-southeast-asia/.

Contributors

BEN BLAND is the director of the Southeast Asia Program at the Lowy Institute and the author of *Man of Contradictions: Joko Widodo and the Struggle to Remake Indonesia* and *Generation HK: Seeking Identity in China's Shadow.* Bland has written a range of papers at the Lowy Institute, including "Politics in Indonesia: Resilient elections, defective democracy" and "Anchoring the Indo-Pacific: The Case for Deeper Australia–India–Indonesia Trilateral Cooperation." He was previously an award-winning correspondent for the *Financial Times* in Indonesia, China, and Vietnam.

DAVID DOLLAR is a senior fellow in the China Center at the Brookings Institution and host of the Dollar & Sense podcast on international trade. He is a leading expert on Asian economies and U.S. relations with Asia. From 2009 to 2013 he was the U.S. Treasury's economic and financial emissary to China, based in Beijing. Before his time at Treasury, Dollar worked at the World Bank for twenty years. He was the country economist for Vietnam during 1989–1995, a period of intense reform and adjustment. From 1995 to 2004, Dollar worked in the World Bank's research department and published articles on trade and growth, economic reform in the developing world, and aid effectiveness. From 2004 to 2009 he was country director for China and Mongolia. Prior to his World Bank career, Dollar was an assistant professor of economics at UCLA, spending a semester in Beijing teaching at the Graduate School of the Chinese Academy of Social Sciences. He has a PhD in economics from NYU and a BA in Asian studies from Dartmouth College.

LINDSEY FORD is a David M. Rubenstein Fellow in the Foreign Policy program at Brookings. Most recently, Ford was the Richard Holbrooke Fellow and director for political-security affairs at the Asia Society Policy Institute (ASPI). From 2009 to 2015, Ford served in a variety of roles within the Office of the Secretary of Defense, including as the special assistant to Secretary of Defense Chuck Hagel for the 2014 U.S.-ASEAN Defense Forum. Most recently, Ford served as the senior adviser to the assistant secretary of defense for Asian and Pacific security affairs, where she managed a team of advisers overseeing maritime security, multilateral security affairs, and force management planning. Ford was also a leading architect of the Asia rebalance strategy work for the Department of Defense's 2012 "Defense Strategic Guidance Review" and oversaw the development of the Department's first "Asia-Pacific Maritime Security Strategy" in 2015.

RICHARD JAVAD HEYDARIAN is an Asia-based scholar, most recently a visiting fellow at National Chengchi University, and formerly assistant professor in political science at De La Salle University. He has written for the world's leading publications, including the *New York Times, Washington Post, The Guardian, Foreign Affairs*, and is a regular contributor to *Aljazeera English, Nikkei Asia, South China Morning Post*, and the *Straits Times*. He has delivered lectures at the world's leading universities, including Harvard, Stanford, and Columbia universities, and is the author of, among other books, *The Rise of Duterte: A Populist Revolt against Elite Democracy* (Palgrave Macmillan, 2017) and *The Indo-Pacific: Trump, China, and the New Struggle for Global Mastery* (Palgrave Macmillan, 2019). He has advised Philippine presidential candidates, presidential cabinet members, senators, and the Armed Forces of the Philippines, and is also a television host in GMA Network in the Philippines.

HERVÉ LEMAHIEU is Director of the Asian Power and Diplomacy Program at the Lowy Institute. Hervé leads the research for the annual Asia Power Index—launched by the Institute in 2018—and authored the methodology to map the changing distribution of power in the region. Hervé joined Lowy from the International Institute for Strategic Studies (IISS) where he was Research Associate for Political Economy and Security, specializing in Southeast Asia. He has also consulted on early warning and geopolitical risk for governments and international organizations. Hervé has an MSc in Global Governance and Diplomacy from the University of Oxford, and an MA in International Relations and Modern History from the University of St Andrews.

THOMAS PEPINSKY is Tisch University Professor in the Department of Government at Cornell University, and nonresident senior fellow at the Brooking Institution. A specialist in Southeast Asian politics, his current research focuses on identity and political economy in a globalized world, and the politics of COVID-19 in the United States and beyond.

ROLAND RAJAH is lead economist and director of the International Economy Program at the Lowy Institute in Sydney, Australia. His research focuses on the Asia-Pacific economies, growth and development issues, international development finance, and geo-economics.

JONATHAN R. STROMSETH is a senior fellow at the Brookings Institution, where he holds the Lee Kuan Yew Chair in Southeast Asia Studies in the Center for East Asia Policy Studies. He also has a joint appointment with the Brookings John L. Thornton China Center. From 2014 to 2017, Stromseth served on the Secretary of State's Policy Planning Staff at the U.S. Department of State, advising the Department's leadership on China, Southeast Asia, and East Asian and Pacific affairs. Previously he was The Asia Foundation's Country Representative to China (2006–2014) and Vietnam (2000–2005), and is a three-time recipient of the Foundation's President's Award for Extraordinary Program Leadership. He holds a doctorate in political science from Columbia University, and is co-author of *China's Governance Puzzle: Enabling Transparency and Participation in a Single-Party State* (Cambridge University Press, 2017). He has also conducted research as a Fulbright Scholar in Singapore, worked for the United Nations peacekeeping operation in Cambodia, and taught Southeast Asian politics at Columbia.

KHUONG VU is an associate professor at the Lee Kuan Yew School of Public Policy at the National University of Singapore. His research and teaching concentrates on strategy and policy issues concerning economic growth, competitiveness, productivity, development strategy, and digital transformation, with a special focus on Asia and ASEAN. Vu has held various government positions in Vietnam, including deputy chief of the Haiphong City Government Office, vice-chairman of the Dinh Vu Economic Zone, and CEO of the state-owned Song Cam Chemical Company. He received a bachelor's degree in mathematics (with highest honors) from Hanoi National University, a Master of Business Administration degree from Harvard Business School, and a doctorate in public policy from Harvard University.

Chronology of the Region
October 2018–November 2020

OCTOBER 5, 2018

The Better Utilization of Investment Leading to Development (BUILD) Act was passed by the U.S. Senate and House of Representatives. It established a new U.S. development agency: the U.S. International Development Finance Corporation (USIDFC). It also doubled the U.S. Overseas Private Investment Corporation's (OPIC) development funding cap to $60 billion worldwide.

NOVEMBER 8, 2018

Australian Prime Minister Scott Morrison delivered his "Australia and the Pacific: A New Chapter" address at the Lavarack Barracks in Townsville, Queensland. The speech highlighted the progress and future endeavors for Australia's national security plans, including its Pacific Step-up policy, which identifies the Pacific Islands as a major foreign policy priority for Australia.

NOVEMBER 12, 2018

The U.S. OPIC, Australia's Department of Foreign Affairs and Trade (DFAT) and Export Finance and Insurance Corporation (EFIC), and the Japan Bank for International Cooperation (JBIC) signed an MOU to launch the Trilateral Partnership for Infrastructure Investment in the Indo-Pacific.

NOVEMBER 11–15, 2018

The 33rd ASEAN Summit was held in Singapore. On the sidelines at the 21st China-ASEAN Summit, the two parties agreed to finalize negotiations on the Code of Conduct for the South China Sea by 2022. They also agreed on an "ASEAN-China Strategic Partnership Vision 2030."

NOVEMBER 14–15, 2018

The 13th East Asia Summit was held in Singapore. On the sidelines, assistant secretary level officials of the Quad met for the third time.

NOVEMBER 16, 2018

U.S. Vice President Mike Pence made a speech at the Asia-Pacific Economic Cooperation (APEC) Summit in Port Moresby, Papua New Guinea, where he further expressed the U.S. government's resolve to address the U.S.-China trade imbalance and the security challenges China poses in the Indo-Pacific.

DECEMBER 31, 2018

President Donald Trump signed the Asia Reassurance Initiative Act (ARIA) into law, which seeks to further develop U.S. policy to address challenges in the Indo-Pacific. ARIA articulates a broader vision of the U.S. commitment to its partners and allies in the Indo-Pacific, including defending security interests, economic interests, and values.

FEBRUARY 27–28, 2019

Leader Kim Jong-un of North Korea and U.S. President Donald Trump conducted their second meeting, this time in Hanoi, Vietnam.

MARCH 24, 2019

General elections were held in Thailand, resulting in a win for the Palang Pracharat Party's coalition, which gained a majority in its Parliament. Thailand's Parliament subsequently reelected the coalition's candidate Prayuth Chan-o-cha as prime minister.

MAY 13, 2019

Midterm elections were held in the Philippines, resulting in President Rodrigo Duterte's allies maintaining their hold on the majority in Congress and their takeover of the majority in the Senate. No opposition politicians won a seat in the Senate.

APRIL 17, 2019

General elections were held in Indonesia, resulting in a reelection win for President Joko Widodo (known as Jokowi). In the legislative elections, Jokowi's Indonesian Democratic Party of Struggle (PDI-P) won the most seats, followed by Prabowo Subianto's Gerindra, then Golkar, the National Awakening Party, the Nasdem Party, and the Prosperous Justice Party.

APRIL 25–27, 2019

The Second Belt and Road Forum was held in Beijing, China, where President Xi Jinping announced $64 billion in new deals.

MAY 31–JUNE 2, 2019

The 18th Asia Security Summit: IISS Shangri-La Dialogue was held in Singapore, where Prime Minister Lee Hsien Loong urged the United States and China to resolve their trade and security issues in his opening remarks. On June 1, then-Acting Secretary of Defense Patrick Shanahan released the U.S. Department of Defense comprehensive "Indo-Pacific Strategy Report."

JUNE 8–9, 2019

The G20 meeting of finance ministers and central bank governors was held in Fukuoka, Japan, where its participants endorsed the new "G20 Principles for Quality Infrastructure Investment," which strives to improve debt sustainability for countries seeking development.

JUNE 26, 2019

Australian Prime Minister Scott Morrison delivered his "Where We Live" foreign policy speech at Asialink, an Australian think tank, in the leadup to the G20 Summit. Prime Minister Morrison's speech reiterated the Australian government's commitment to maintaining regional stability and prosperity in the Indo-Pacific.

JUNE 28–29, 2019

The G20 Summit was held in Osaka, Japan, where leaders discussed trade, climate change, and other matters. On the sidelines, President Donald Trump and Prime Ministers Shinzo Abe and Narendra Modi met for the 2nd Japan-America-India Trilateral Dialogue to discuss improved connectivity and infrastructure development in the Indo-Pacific.

JUNE 20–23, 2019

The 34th ASEAN Summit was held in Bangkok, Thailand, where ASEAN released its "ASEAN Outlook on the Indo-Pacific," which stressed the importance of ASEAN centrality and also called for ASEAN-led mechanisms like the East Asia Summit to serve as platforms for discussions on Indo-Pacific cooperation.

AUGUST 1, 2019

At the 10th annual Lower Mekong Initiative Ministerial meeting in Bangkok, Thailand, U.S. Secretary of State Mike Pompeo announced the launch of the Japan-U.S. Mekong Power Partnership (JUMPP), which aims to develop the Lower Mekong's regional electricity grids with the U.S. initial commitment of $29.5 million under Asia EDGE, along with a commitment to countering transnational crime and trafficking with the U.S. initial commitment of $14 million.

SEPTEMBER 26, 2019

The Foreign Ministers of the Quad met for the first time on the sidelines of the 74th UN General Assembly.

OCTOBER 31–NOVEMBER 4, 2019

The 35th ASEAN Summit was held in Bangkok, Thailand, where U.S. National Security Advisor Robert O'Brien delivered President Donald

Trump's invitation to the ASEAN leaders for a special summit in the United States in the first quarter of 2020.

NOVEMBER 4, 2019

The 2019 Indo-Pacific Business Forum was held in Bangkok, Thailand, where the United States, Australia, and Japan announced the establishment of a trilateral development initiative, "The Blue Dot Network." The three partners seek to support development opportunities in the region, as well as promote global trust standards and responsible development. The U.S. Department of State also released its "A Free and Open Indo-Pacific" report at this forum, summarizing the implementation of two years of U.S. diplomatic, economic, governance, and security initiatives in the Indo-Pacific region.

NOVEMBER 4, 2019

The 14th East Asia Summit was held in Bangkok, Thailand. On the sidelines of the East Asia Summit, senior officials from the foreign ministries of Australia, India, Japan, and the United States met to further discuss collaboration through the Quad in counterterrorism, cyber issues, development finance, maritime security, humanitarian assistance, and disaster response.

NOVEMBER 4, 2019

The 3rd Regional Comprehensive Economic Partnership (RCEP) Summit was held in Bangkok, Thailand, where it was declared that fifteen of the original sixteen members had concluded the text-based negotiations on an RCEP free-trade pact. India decided not to join RCEP at this time due to protectionist concerns. The RCEP deal was then expected to be signed in late 2020.

DECEMBER 18, 2019

The third India-Australia-Indonesia Trilateral Senior Officials' Dialogue was held in New Delhi. Previous meetings were held in Canberra (2018) and Bogor (2017). Foreign Affairs ministers of each party discussed their foreign policy objectives, including the ASEAN Indo-Pacific Outlook and India's Indo-Pacific Oceans Initiative, and general developments in the Indo-Pacific and in regional forums. They also agreed to hold a fourth meeting sometime in 2020.

JANUARY 17, 2020

The ASEAN Foreign Ministers' Retreat was held in Hanoi, Vietnam, where the ASEAN Foreign Ministers discussed President Donald Trump's invitation for a special U.S.-ASEAN summit in Las Vegas on March 14. All ten members of ASEAN agreed to participate in the summit, though Philippine President Rodrigo Duterte and Malaysian Prime Minister Mahathir Mohamed stated that they would send representatives in their stead.

FEBRUARY 28, 2020

The Trump administration announced that the special U.S.-ASEAN summit in Las Vegas was postponed due to growing concerns regarding the spread of COVID-19.

MARCH 1, 2020

Malaysian Prime Minister Muhyiddin Yassin took power, after an internal political coup led by members of the Malaysian United Indigenous Party (Bersatu) and leaders of the National Front (Barisan Nasional) forced Prime Minister Mahathir to resign and ousted the coalition government of Pakatan Harapan on February 23.

MARCH 11, 2020

The World Health Organization declared COVID-19 a pandemic.

APRIL 13, 2020

Eyes on Earth Inc. published findings in a U.S.-government funded study that China's upstream dams are impounding much more water from the downstream, exacerbating the severe drought in the Lower Mekong basin. China immediately dismissed these findings. The Mekong River Commission, an intergovernmental body that works in managing the Lower Mekong basin, called for greater data transparency from China after the report was released.

APRIL 14, 2020

Vietnam, which had assumed the ASEAN Chairmanship in the midst of the COVID-19 pandemic, hosted a virtual Special ASEAN Summit on Coronavirus Disease 2019 (COVID-19), convening the leaders of ASEAN to discuss their concerns regarding its negative impacts on the well-being of the people and global socioeconomic developments. Vietnam then hosted a Special ASEAN Plus Three Summit on Coronavirus Disease 2019 (COVID-19) to discuss these concerns with the leaders of China, Japan, and South Korea.

APRIL 26, 2020
The United States and Laos Co-hosted a Special ASEAN-United States Foreign Ministers' Meeting on Coronavirus Disease 2019 (COVID-19).

APRIL 29, 2020
U.S. Secretary of State Mike Pompeo announced that the State Department will be requiring a Clean Path for all 5G network traffic entering and exiting U.S. diplomatic facilities. The 5G Clean Path features an end-to-end communication path that does not use any transmission, control, computing, or storage equipment from IT vendors such as Huawei and ZTE that are required to comply with directives of the Chinese Communist Party.

APRIL 30, 2020
A Special Video Conference of Health Ministers of ASEAN and The United States in Enhancing Cooperation on Coronavirus Disease 2019 (Covid-19) Response was held.

MAY 4, 2020
U.S. Under Secretary for Economic Growth, Energy, and the Environment Keith Krach stated that the U.S. government is seeking to establish an alliance of trusted partners in the wake of the COVID-19 pandemic called the "Economic Prosperity Network," according to Reuters. It would include companies and civil society groups operating under the same set of standards for matters pertaining to digital business, energy, infrastructure, research, trade, education, and commerce. In a press briefing on April 29, where Secretary of State Pompeo elaborated on the Clean Path announcement, he said the U.S. government is "working with our friends in Australia, in India, in Japan, New Zealand, Republic of Korea, and Vietnam to share information and best practices as we begin to move the global economy forward."

MAY 26, 2020

The government of Japanese Prime Minister Shinzo Abe passed a $1.1 trillion stimulus package to combat the financial pains of the COVID-19 pandemic. The stimulus makes subsidies available to Japanese companies to shift production out of China into Southeast Asia, as well as back to Japan, to protect from the ensuing supply chain disruptions.

JUNE 26, 2020

The 36th ASEAN Summit, previously scheduled for April 2020, was held online on this date due to the COVID-19 pandemic. Here, the leaders established a new ASEAN Covid-19 response fund to meet urgent needs during epidemics.

JULY 13, 2020

U.S. Secretary of State Mike Pompeo released a press statement announcing that the United States now explicitly aligns its position with the 2016 South China Sea Arbitration ruling that rejected China's maritime claims outside of its EEZ and continental shelf as having no basis in international law. In doing so, the United States declared China's claims and activities across most of the South China Sea to be "unlawful" for the first time.

JULY 23, 2020

U.S. Secretary of State Mike Pompeo delivered a speech at the Richard Nixon Presidential Library titled "Communist China and the Free World's Future," declaring U.S. engagement with China a failure and urging countries to pressure the Chinese Communist Party to change its behavior.

AUGUST 5, 2020

U.S. Secretary of State Mike Pompeo announced the Clean Network, an expansion of the Clear Path directive announced on April 29. The announcement said U.S. internet infrastructure will exclude Chinese telecoms firms, apps, and cloud providers. It also invited governments and industry partners around the world to join. Indo-Pacific countries included in a U.S. Department of State factsheet list of like-minded Clean Countries and Territories are Japan, Taiwan, and Vietnam. The list of "Clean Telcos" in the Indo-Pacific include Jio in India, Telstra in Australia, SK and KT in

South Korea, NTT in Japan, Singtel in Singapore, and "all the 5G telcos" in Vietnam and Taiwan.

AUGUST 24, 2020

The 3rd Lancang-Mekong Cooperation summit was held online with leaders from China and the Lower Mekong countries. Prime Minister Li Keqiang pledged to share more water management data from its portion of the Mekong River with its neighbors downstream, though the details of this pledge were unclear.

SEPTEMBER 8, 2020

Laos's state-owned Electricite du Laos (EdL) and China's state-owned China Southern Power Grid Co. (CSPGC) signed a power grid shareholding deal. The deal established the joint venture, Electricite du Laos Transmission Company Limited (EDLT) and ceded majority control of Laos' electric grid to the Chinese company.

SEPTEMBER 9, 2020

U.S. Secretary of State Mike Pompeo participated in the virtual ASEAN-United States Foreign Ministers meeting, where he told ASEAN foreign ministers to stand up against China's policies in the Mekong sub-region and South China Sea. He went on to say, "Don't let the Chinese Communist Party walk over us and our people. You should have confidence and the American will be here in friendship to help you."

SEPTEMBER 11, 2020

U.S. Deputy Secretary of State Stephen Beigun and the Foreign Ministers of ASEAN countries launched the Mekong-U.S. Partnership at the first Mekong-U.S. Partnership Ministerial Meeting held online. This new Partnership acts as a strategic forum for cooperation and expands on the work done by the Lower Mekong Initiative established during the Obama administration.

SEPTEMBER 16, 2020

Yoshihide Suga took over as Japan's Prime Minister after being elected following Prime Minister Shinzo Abe's stepped down due to health concerns.

Prime Minister Suga later decided to visit Vietnam and Indonesia in October as his first trip abroad in his new role, demonstrating the resolve of the Japanese government to continue close engagement with its Southeast Asian partners. Also, on this day, France, the UK, and Germany submitted a joint Note Verbale to the United Nations against China's South China Sea claims.

SEPTEMBER 26, 2020

The Sabah state elections were held in Malaysia, resulting in a victory for Prime Minister Muhyiddin Yassin's ruling coalition. This victory was believed to strengthen Muhyiddin's position in the face of the leadership challenge posed by the opposition leader Anwar Ibrahim.

OCTOBER 6, 2020

The Foreign Ministers of the Quad met in Tokyo, the first standalone meeting of the Quad, with previous iterations happening in the background of other regional summits. U.S. Secretary of State Pompeo was explicit in condemning China at the meeting, asking Quad partners to collaborate against "the CCP's exploitation, corruption and coercion."

NOVEMBER 8, 2020

General elections were held in Myanmar, resulting in a landslide victory for the ruling National League for Democracy (NLD) party, which won 396 seats out of the 664-seat bicameral parliament, six more seats than it had won in its electoral victory in 2015.

NOVEMBER 12–15, 2020

The 37th ASEAN Summit was held online. There, the ASEAN members adopted the ASEAN Comprehensive Recovery Framework (ACRF) exit strategy for the COVID-19 pandemic, as well as its Implementation Plan.

NOVEMBER 15, 2020

The 4th RCEP Summit was held via video conference, where its fifteen members signed the world's largest trade agreement.

Trilateral Dialogue Participants and Observers

ASEAN, Australia, United States

October 29–30, 2019, Grand Copthorne Waterfront, Singapore

* Denotes participants who authored a paper

DELEGATION FROM THE BROOKINGS INSTITUTION/THE UNITED STATES

DAVID DOLLAR*
Senior Fellow
The Brookings Institution

LINDSEY FORD*
David M. Rubenstein Fellow
The Brookings Institution

BRUCE JONES
Vice President & Director of the
Foreign Policy Program
The Brookings Institution

THOMAS PARKS
Country Representative for Thailand
The Asia Foundation

THOMAS PEPINSKY*
Professor of Government
Cornell University

MIREYA SOLIS
Senior Fellow and Director of the
Center for East Asia Policy Studies
The Brookings Institution

JONATHAN R. STROMSETH
Senior Fellow and Lee Kuan Yew
Chair in Southeast Asian Studies
The Brookings Institution

DELEGATION FROM THE LOWY INSTITUTE/AUSTRALIA

BEN BLAND*
Director of the Southeast Asia
Project
Lowy Institute

MALCOM COOK
Senior Fellow
Institute of Southeast Asian Studies

HUONG LE THU
Senior Analyst of the Defence
and Strategy Program
Australian Strategic Policy Institute

JOHN LEE
Senior Fellow at the United States
Studies Centre
University of Sydney

HERVE LEMAHIEU*
Director of the Asian Power and
Diplomacy Program
Lowy Institute

RICHARD MCGREGOR
Senior Fellow
Lowy Institute

ROLAND RAJAH*
Director of the International
Economy
Program
Lowy Institute

GREG RAYMOND
Research Fellow
Australian National University

EVE WARBURTON
Postdoctoral Fellow
National University of Singapore

DELEGATION FROM RSIS/ASEAN

MELY CABALLERO-ANTHONY
Head of the Centre for Non-
Traditional Security Studies
*S. Rajaratnam School of
International Studies*

TERMSAK CHALERMPALANUPAP
Lead Researcher at the ASEAN
Studies Centre
Institute of Southeast Asian Studies

RICHARD HEYDARIAN*
Research Fellow
National Chengchi University

COLLIN KOH SWEE LEAN
Research Fellow at the Institute of
Defense and Strategic Studies
*S. Rajaratnam School of
International Studies*

JOSEPH LIOW
Research Adviser and Tan Kah
Kee Chair in Comparative and
International Politics
*S. Rajaratnam School of
International Studies*

NGUYEN HUNG SON
Bien Dong Institute for Maritime
Studies
Diplomatic Academy of Vietnam

KAREN PITAKDUMRONGKIT
Deputy Head of the Center for
Multilateralism Studies
*S. Rajaratnam School of
International Studies*

CHARLOTTE SETIJADI
Assistant Professor of Humanities
Singapore Management University

PHILIPS VERMONTE*
Executive Director
Center for Strategic and International Studies / Jakarta

KHUONG MINH VU*
Associate Professor
Lee Kuan Yew School of Public Policy

WILLIAM CHOONG
Shangri-La Dialogue Senior Fellow
for Asia-Pacific Security
International Institute for Strategic Studies - Asia

H.E. BARRY DESKER
Distinguished Fellow and Former
Ambassador
S. Rajaratnam School of International Studies

RALF EMMERS
Dean and President's Chair in
International Relations
S. Rajaratnam School of International Studies

NICOLAS FANG
Director of Security and Global
Affairs
Singapore Institute of International Affairs

KHUONG YUEN FOONG
Vice Dean and Li Ka Shing Professor
in Political Science
Lee Kuan Yew School of Public Policy

ZIAD HAIDER
Senior Associate and Simon Chair in
Political Economy
Center for Strategic and International Studies

CHARMAINE WILLOUGHBY
Associate Professor in the
Department of International Studies
De La Salle University

SELINA HO
Assistant Professor and Program
Chair
Lee Kuan Yew School of Public Policy

C RAJA MOHAN
Director of the Institute of Southeast
Asian Studies
National University of Singapore

DALJIT SINGH
Senior Fellow and Coordinator in
the Regional Strategic and Political
Science Programme
Institute of Southeast Asian Studies

SARAH TEO
Associate Research Fellow in the
Regional Security Architecture
Programme
S. Rajaratnam School of International Studies

YEO LAY HWEE
Adjunct Fellow
Nanyang Technical University

OBSERVERS: ASEAN

LIEW CHIN TONG (KEYNOTE)
Deputy Minister of Defence of
Malaysia

ADRIAN ANG (RAPPORTEUR)
Research Fellow in the U.S.
Programme
*S. Rajaratnam School of
International Studies*

AMANDA TREA PHUA (RAPPORTEUR)
Senior Analyst, U.S. Programme
*S. Rajaratnam School of
International Studies*

OBSERVERS: AUSTRALIA

SOPHIA MCINTYRE
Assistant Secretary of the Southeast
Asia Regional Engagement Branch
*Southeast Asia Division, Department
of Foreign Affairs and Trade,
Australia*

KATE DUFF
Deputy High Commissioner
*Australian High Commission,
Singapore*

NICHOLAS KAY
First Secretary
*Australian High Commission,
Singapore*

OBSERVERS: JAPAN

KAORI HAYASHI
Senior Representative in Singapore
*Japan Bank for International
Cooperation*

TAKASHI KOMORI
Advisor, Office for Peace Building
and Reconstruction
*Infrastructure and Peacebuilding
Department, Japan International
Cooperation Agency*

Index

CPSIA information can be obtained
at www.ICGtesting.com
Printed in the USA
LVHW020257230221
679551LV00001B/1